How To Avoid Going Broke!

A PRIMER *for*

Parents

and

Their Teenagers

By

Matthew Rich

Printed in the United States of America

First Printing, 2020

Table of Contents

For caring parents needing help to teach their teenagers about getting into and out of debt wisely!

PREFACE

The moment your youngster begins to have a need for formal use of money is an important turning point in parenting. As a parent, it is very important to properly prepare your child for that oncoming stage in his or her life. Equally important; to guide them through it you need to be well prepared yourself. As a caring parent you want to do the best job possible. Not all parents are ready for that responsibility and many of them need help in achieving it.

How to Avoid Going Broke!* A Primer for Parents and *Their Teenagers is the second in Matthew Rich's ongoing sequence of primers being written to enable parents to begin teaching their children the fundamentals of money management. The first book in the series is ***How to Borrow Money! Handle Credit! Repay Debt!* BASIC LESSONS *for Parents and Their Children.***

Lots of books have been published on the many money management needs of a typical lifetime. What is unique about this series of primers?

Your youngster is not facing lifetime needs. Car buying and car leasing, taking out a home mortgage, paying for higher education etc. have not surfaced yet in his or her world. Investing in stocks, bonds, gold etc. and retirement planning and saving are well beyond the horizon. When those adult-age needs start happening; your mature child can access a wide range of comprehensive, in-depth books written by professional financial planners. That will come in due time.

Right now, your youngster needs informed parental help. And parents cherish the insight and experienced knowledge of other parents who already have walked along the path successfully. All the better if any of the other parents is a capable teacher. Matthew Rich offers such invaluable experience and capability.

Rich's primers focus specifically on helping parents tutor their young kids about how to handle money wisely. They provide compact guidance and information that parents can utilize from the outset of their young child's formal debt needs. The intent of the books is to foster parents and their children to work together as each debt situation arises. Almost certainly the first foray will be a plea for a credit or debit card! It might happen like this.

Entering the house your teenager daughter calls out, "Hey Mom! Dad! Are you home?" On the sofa, back to her, Dad slowly turns his seated body and acknowledges. "Yes, I'm right here sweetie. What do you want?" She chimes out, "Some of my older friends in the senior class came back this year with a credit card. They were bragging about it. I never thought about it but now I am sort of envious of them. We have never talked about credit cards. I don't know anything about them. I guess I will eventually need one, so can you explain them to me? Then maybe I can get one too? Maybe right away!"

The author has published two in-depth books in his other book series entitled **DEBT is a Four-Letter Word - *But it Need Not Be!*** They help parents, their children, and young people in general to effectively maneuver through first-time debt worries. Chronologically, the books cover aspects of formal debt need and issues that occur as a young person grows from about the age of 16 to around the age of 35. Written in narrative style, fictional Nicole and Dad jointly navigate through her debt needs from her teen years, college years, and onward. The reader observes their monetary processes and outcomes and how Dad interacts with her caringly and effectively and builds both her receptiveness, trust, and self-reliance. Matthew Rich's primers serve as condensed preludes to those extended books.

How to Borrow Money! Handle Credit! Repay Debt!* BASIC LESSONS *for Parents and Their Children serves as a soft-landing vehicle for you to share with your child when formal debt needs first begin to surface. It covers the basics parts, nuts, and bolts of generally taking on formal debt and how it is repaid. It illustrates the problems created when debt is either not properly repaid or unscrupulous circumstances exist in the terms of a loan. The monetary aspects of taking on and repaying debt from credit cards is explained. "Amortization" and repayment of "amortized" loans are explained and illustrated via numerical examples.

HOW TO AVOID GOING BROKE! *A Primer for Parents and Their Teenagers* describes what it means to be broke, its implications and how to avoid it happening to you. You will:

- learn strategies for routinely saving money that work, including adopting the Golden Rule for Saving!
- be able to overcome your resistance to making a budget for your income!

- learn how to create an accurate monthly budget, on the fly!
- use your budget to steadily save money for your priorities.
- be able to face and resolve family money matters calmly and in a cooperative way.

Above all, using the approaches taught in this primer, you be able to regularly afford to "smell the roses" and enjoy fun activities, without worries and monetary stress.

BACKGROUND

As a professor in civil engineering, teaching, and advising students was a large part of my heartbeat. Helping them hone their technical talents and launch professional careers was my endearing commitment. As a researcher, I managed millions of dollars in research contracts and grants. Aside that, I guided numerous graduate students to utilize and manage portions of the budget available from my funded research projects. If they ran out of money, they would be in trouble. Yet, with proper oversight, that never happened. Now retired from teaching, it was with that same vigor and care that I undertook writing books for parents and their children to use in managing everyday debt matters.

My professional evolution in budget management led me to transfer those highly developed skills into the domestic environment. Computer-based tools I homed in on at work found their way into managing home finances. They enabled invaluable tracking of income and expenses, producing periodic account summaries, budget status, expenditure projections and so forth. Indeed, those very tools served to produce all the numerical content in my books. With these tools at hand, my wife and I grew to manage finances and debt in a strongly cooperative and coordinated way.

My teenaged daughter brought typical youthful challenges regarding handling money. Getting a teenager's attention to listen to a parent trying to offer advice on anything is trying. Taking on discussions of managing money was way down on her list of things to do. Gaining her receptivity was like walking a desert and hoping to find water. With persistence and patience, I managed to gain her attention and trust to let me help her out with money matters. Little by little she learned about the ins and outs of credit cards, bank loans, auto loans, student loans, home mortgages and other common types of loans.

I shared how, when I was young like her, I had some naiveté, unawareness, and a degree of indifference about formally borrowing and paying back money. I was ignorant about exactly how to prepare for and make decisions about borrowing money. I also had plenty of the negative surprises that debt can, and does, put into one's life. When I learned to dig into and understand the details, I began to make better decisions and do it faster and more effectively.

Over time, my daughter evolved from disinterest in monetary matters and reluctance for advice to asking for my help on all important money matters. Now a young adult, she is much better, well prepared personal money manager and successful business owner. I still get occasional requests from her when unfamiliar territory comes along, and it is always endearing to receive them and help her out!

In retirement, I am converting my lifetime of hard knocks, bad and good experiences, and subsequent growth in family debt management into a powerful sequence of lessons I learned and now am sharing through my books. They reflect my incisive evolution about debt acquisition and management, and my developed techniques and strategies to astutely deal with debt needs at all stages of life. They are written from the perspective of a parent who walked the talk of his own personal experience with his child and a teacher wanting to help other parents do likewise.

Reading my primers constitutes the first (perhaps, baby) steps parents can take to instill basic debt management in their children during their formative teenage years and beyond. They helped me with my daughter. Now, let me begin helping you with your child.

Lesson 1

Nobody Knows You When You're Broke!

What does it mean to be "broke"?

Privately, one of your buddies tells you "I'm broke!" What are you to make of his admission? Seems straight-forward, he does not have any money. Definition-wise, a Merriam-Webster dictionary agrees, going broke means "to spend or lose all of one's money". At closer look, it is more vague than specific. Exactly what is "one's money" that has vanished? There are lots of possibilities:

He is living paycheck to paycheck and has entirely spent the most recent one. In addition, he has no other monetary resources (savings). The next paycheck will provide relief only for whatever time it takes to spend it. His "broke" is barely passing through each month being penniless and scared.

Or your buddy was terminated from his manual job due to technology replacing him. He is broke because there is no incoming money. He is worried how long his savings will last and if his job skill is an extinct need.

Or it could be that after spending on necessities, he owes more on loans than he can pay monthly. He is overspent and spiraling into being broke. Oh, but he has a speedboat and a new muscle car sitting in the driveway. His form of broke is "the banks own me" but he enjoys his toys. He could sell them but prefers to remain broke according to his terms.

Or he is divorced, paying exorbitant alimony, and blames his ex for being broke.

Or his savings and assets were wiped out by losing a lawsuit over an injury caused to a plaintiff in an auto accident. His sense of broke is having 'lost everything' because of a jury.

Or he went for broke in a risky investment which

failed. Still has income and assets, but no savings. His broke is his empty bank account.

Or he retired early without a pension and a serious health care problem arose. The expenses are overwhelming his retirement savings. His form of broke is his certainty that his savings will be spent entirely, and his illiquid assets (home, automobile, furnishings) attacked by creditors. In his mind all those events have already occurred.

How can one handle be being broke?

Whatever the nature of being broke, there are financial and emotional outcomes. Address both.

If literally penniless, it likely means tapping government safety net services. Before doing so, write a contract with one's self agreeing to stop after a fixed period of the shortest, comfortable duration. To confront a likely feeling of loss of dignity; swallow your pride, take the step, and share it and the reasons for it with a few trusted friends.

If not literally penniless in terms of currency, take stock of what assets remain. Why have they been untouched? Overcome the reasons and start to use some of them to recover.

Depending on the severity, sell or rent that nice house and purchase or rent a more affordable alternative residence. For sure, sell that boat. Trade in that muscle car for a leased everyday economy car. Spread the gain out over coming months by living a Spartan lifestyle. Compensate by starting a physical fitness regimen.

Out of work? Start seeking employment.

Your risky investment tanked? Likely you knew the risk, accepted it, and can take the loss in stride. If not, vow to never repeat it.

Suddenly going broke can hit you hard!

Going broke can happen suddenly. If it does, it can hit hard and leave you reeling.

Loss of blue-collar employment due to a lack of technology skills can require training and education to qualify elsewhere.

Loss of white-collar employment at a later age due to

a company suddenly scaling down or being sold occurs frequently. And, the reality is, being older makes job hunting for a similarly paying position very challenging.

Put aside that thought of borrowing money to dig out. Being unemployed and/or having low net worth will severely hinder, if not prevent, you from borrowing money. If you manage to borrow some, expect a very high rate of interest.

Events such as paying huge injury damages to a plaintiff crippled after she slipped on the ice on your sidewalk will have sudden and long-term financial consequences. Likely, you will face loss of your home and long-term compensation payments to the plaintiff. Psychologically, guilt and depression are genuine threats.

"Nobody knows you when you down and out.
In my pocket, not one penny.
And my friends I haven't any."

Written by Jimmy Cox in 1923, those lyrics have rung true ever since. Being broke, you will lose contact with lots of people in your circle of friends and acquaintances.

NOTE: "you" is grammatically incorrect but quoted exactly as was written in the source. Several other cases occur in subsequent quotations of other lyrics from the song.

How can one avoid going broke?

Avoiding being broke requires leading a financially responsible life. Saving money is the first step. If you are constantly unable to save money, then you are digging deeper toward the risk of going broke. Without reserves, high-cost monetary surprises can cause you to break through and go broke.

Lots of people experience a feeling of always having to "make ends meet." Further cutting **take-home pay** by regular withdrawals for savings feels impossible. Subsequently, I cover how to implement ***My Golden Rule of Saving: Pay Yourself Last, But Always Pay Yourself Something!*** Following the advice and steps described in it will guide you to saving money as a regular habit.

Living within one's means is vital. Having an accurate

budget is the start. Month to month tracking of spending and adjusting discretionary spending on the fly, leads to correctly controlled outlays and homing in on a realistic **MONTHLY budget** over time. Keeping to it helps develop the discipline needed to overcome the temptation of **impulsive frivolous purchases**. In ***LESSON 4 Budgets and Budget Busters*** *and* ***LESSON 5 Creating an Accurate MONTH Budget – On the Fly*** I detail how to go about creating a budget.

Auto insurance, health insurance, life insurance, and the like can keep you and your family members from going broke. It is especially important to have adequate insurance for unlikely, but possible, events such as being sued by that person who slips on the ice on your sidewalk or walkway. Retirement life will be much smoother with long-term care insurance in place.

Keeping current with technology is costly. Cell phones and computers regularly require upgrading to newer, faster, more versatile models. Cell phone service, internet service and website fees are very pricey. There are pulls in ads and comments from friends that tend to make you feel that you have outdated equipment and devices. Being realistic about such costs and containing them will save you a lot of money.

Pursuing a college education places a heavy strain on financial resources. It is very expensive. And the cost is rising rapidly. Whether well-defined yet or not, your child's career aspirations versus the affordability of potential colleges to attend are at the forefront. Many students and parents, even those who have saved for the costs, end up taking out loans.

The author (a parent and retired professor) has published an extensive book on the subject, **DEBT is a Four-Letter Word - *But it Need Not Be!* THE COLLEGE EXPERIENCE**. In the United States, the average student loan debt for college graduates is nearing $30,000. Often, the student's parents borrow even more atop that. Annual rates of interest on federal student loans are higher than current home mortgage rates. For parents, the annual rates of interest approach twice that level. Parents should aim for the most affordable college that fits the child's academic area of interest and is the best fit for cost, location, and success upon graduation. Start financially preparing for future costs as soon as the child is born or even before.

Jimmy Cox continued with,

"But If I ever get on my feet again
Then I'll meet my long-lost friend"

Undoubtedly, you never want to find yourself having to worry about being down and out and having no friends. By reading this book, you will learn how to handle money effectively and avoid such misery. You will enhance your ability to pay your bills and save for future needs. And, you will have discretionary money for things you want and activities to do that will ease the journey and put fun into your life!

LESSON 2

The Starting Line for Having Fun: Saving Money

What is one to do when after paying all the bills there is nothing left for the fun things in life? You want to travel. You want to attend a major sports event. Fill in the blank: You want to ______. Lacking spare funds or facing debt needs and worries amidst a wish list of need-to-do and like-to-do things is not fun at all! Getting out of that ditch and affording to enjoy some "smell the roses" activities takes a game plan. I have one and its play book works. I will be sharing the plays in it.

Saving money is the starting line in my game plan. Let's start moving down the field.

<u>Most</u> people realize that money does not grow on trees and <u>seldom</u> falls from the sky. I say "most" because I have encountered people who seem to behave as if it does. They believe in the phrase "it came out of the blue", alternative wording for "it fell from the sky." My use of "seldom" is also intentional. An accident might cause some cash to fly out of a

security vehicle. However, if retrieved, it is best you return it. The currency can be readily tracked. If you do not return it, you could end up reading this book while confined in jail.

After all the unrealistic and extraordinary sources for obtaining cash are considered it settles in that one must accumulate cash by the quite ordinary act of saving it. A dependable routine for steadily building up a reserve of cash is essential. That reserve permits one to pay for anticipated larger needs of life by planned accumulation of savings for timely availability. At an early age, there is that "piggy bank". With mine, I learned a valuable lesson. Saving coins at a regular monthly increase in the incremental amount resulted in my stowaway cash growing faster and faster. I have heeded it all my life.

Later in life it was replaced by the so-called "penny jar" whereby one regularly puts one's pennies into a large jar. It gave important lessons, too. It is more effective to regularly put in all of one's loose coins. Add any windfall money to that. The sort that seems to "fall from the sky," meaning it comes about unexpectedly. Things like a $10.00 rebate for buying a backpack and a $100.00 rebate for buying a camera were fed into mine. Occasional monetary gifts, occasional winnings from a bet on a horse race, income tax refunds, etc. were plopped in. If left in, after a year or two that penny jar would contain several hundred to several thousand dollars. I did not let it burn a hole in my pocket.

Let's turn down the path to more programmatic, adult approaches to seriously saving money. A locked-in regular bank savings pattern is the first action to take. If controlled effectively, then long-term financial needs can be successfully managed via tapping accumulated savings wisely. If it is planned properly, then even when occasional expenditures are made using them the remaining reserves will continue to increase.

One approach to regularly saving money is to arrange for a consistent amount of money from your paycheck to be automatically deposited into a bank savings account. Those much larger adult age savings will accumulate at a steady rate. As pay raises occur, consider increasing the percentage to be taken out. That way, the savings will grow faster and faster.

Again, this is most reliable if you never withdraw any of those funds.

The other side of the savings spectrum is to control one's spending. Controlling expenses is the most important step toward minimizing personal debt. Minimizing personal debt allows maximizing personal savings. Control spending like a wise miser!

For some readers, maintaining a bank savings pattern is a daunting obstacle, not an open gate to paradise. Again, lots of us have experienced a feeling of having to "make ends meet". With every paycheck, withholdings for taxes, and government retirement programs, etc. have reduced the **MONTHLY** gross pay to a lower **MONTHLY** take-home pay amount. That is the base amount from which to manage one's daily, weekly, monthly, and annual financial needs.

Typically, one then acts to pay outstanding bills and hopes to have money left over to devote to optional spending. That can leave you feeling "there is never any money left over after paying all the bills". The idea of enacting regular withdrawals for savings feels insurmountable if not impossible. By following my game plan, you will overcome that. Here are the first few plays. My game plan starts with having two separate bank savings accounts and they always get a deposit at the end of each month.

The **Primary Savings Account** is used to accumulate funds for known regularly needed purchases of higher cost. It also serves to steadily increase savings for possible long-term needs. Medical, dental and eye care examinations and ensuing costs such as eyeglasses exemplify regularly needed purchases. Clothing, shoes, gifts and other holiday costs, and insurance premiums are other common items. Saving for a down payment on a first-time home mortgage loan is a long-term cost. Homeowners also incur ongoing maintenance costs such as lawn and tree care services. Down the road you will have expenses like painting the house and replacing the roof shingles.

The **Rainy-Day Savings Account** serves as base of money in reserve to pay for periodic unexpected and emergency needs, and periodic expenditures for “smelling the roses”. A Rainy-Day for finances is a day that interrupts the sunny days of life with an event that costs a significant amount of money. Paying the deductible amounts on a major medical emergency and auto accident insurance claims, failure of a water heater, and removal of a dying large tree are examples of big raindrops.

My play book handles travel costs (going on a vacation, attending a wedding or college graduation, etc.) by the tandem of my Primary Savings Account and my Rainy-Day Savings Account. Costs for a rental car, airline tickets, hotel, and a gift are taken from my Rainy-Day Savings Account. Restaurant meals and other large "on the fly" costs are taken from my Primary Savings Account. Incidental costs are paid by cash, check or a credit/debit card and absorbed without use of savings.

As to "smelling the roses", what is a rose? A rose is anything that fits in the context of either "splurging" for gratification (satisfying a feeling of "I earned it") or for periodic escapes from the doldrums of everyday life. Celebrating a major wedding anniversary; attending a professional sports event or concert, and weekend getaways are example roses. In a pinch, the smell the roses funds can also serve to put a smile on one's face when using cash instead of a loan to purchase something.

So, all is rosy now? Not really. In the next ***LESSON*** we will move closer! In it I explain my *Golden Rule for Saving*. Start imagining some roses to smell. Down the road, you will be doing it!

Lesson 3

My Golden Rule of Saving: Pay Yourself Last, But Always Pay Yourself Something!

Roses, roses everywhere, but you have no spare money to sniff them.

To store up money for optional, fun needs, many planners say, "Pay yourself first, and then pay your bills". Take money out of your paycheck for discretionary wants at the outset and then take on the bills. To my thinking that causes problems.

When you pay yourself first, you can overpay yourself! If you do overpay yourself, then you will be unable to fully pay off your bills. If that continues, then your unpaid bills become a heavier and heavier burden, even daunting. Eventually those bills will seem insurmountable, and they will be. You will begin to be contacted by bill collection agencies. Then, chances are you will never have money to "smell the roses". Instead, you will be getting deeper and deeper into the weeds.

Likely, your bills reflect spending on some unwise, impulsive needs. That is why I do not rely entirely on the "Pay yourself first, and then pay your bills" approach. Instead, I advocate you also practice the opposite approach, "Pay yourself *last*, but always pay yourself *something*". It is my ***Golden Rule of Saving***.

Assume I am just beginning the process. On the first day of the month, my paycheck for the preceding month arrives by electronic deposit to my bank checking account. The amount is my **MONTHLY** take-home pay. At that time, I put a fixed amount of money into my **Primary Savings Account**. The fixed amount is what I anticipate I'll be able to transfer each month as Regular Savings amount!

Then, my usual monthly bills are paid as they arrive in

the mail. A few are automatic payments arranged via my bank. Loan payments and insurance premiums are two examples. I limit automatic payments because if they are overlooked it messes up my checkbook accounting.

With very rare exceptions, at the end of the month there are some funds left in my checking account. Let's refer to them as the **End of the Month** (**EOM**) funds.

Once my <u>next</u> paycheck has been electronically deposited into my checking account, I transfer one half of the **EOM** funds to my **Primary Savings Account** and the other half to my **Rainy-Day Savings Account**. For example, if the remaining amount is $200, then I deposit $100 into each account. That insures that at the end of every month, I have acted to "Pay myself <u>last</u>, but pay myself something".

Each succeeding month I add the **½ EOM** funds to **Primary Savings Account** until I accumulate a target minimum balance to sustain. That is an estimated upper limit for larger expenses anticipated to occur over some comfortable period, perhaps during the coming 5 years. The amount above that base is used for long-term needs such as retirement and funeral expenses I aim to get the extra amount to a desired level over a reasonable period. It may drop off from time to time but be recoverable and growing overall.

Then I add the other **½ EOM** funds to the **Rainy-Day Savings Account** continuously to accumulate a target minimum balance, too. That is an estimated upper limit for surprise larger expenses that are likely to occur over a year or so. Once the base amount needed is reached, the growing excess funds are available for "smell the roses" activities. I can use them when the moments feel right. The amount of excess funds will fluctuate up and down as those moments come and go. But I am sniffing those roses!

As a reference point, assume that an individual has modest cash in his or her present savings account and wants to begin accumulating more. Consider that account as the **Primary Savings Account**. Act to set up a **Rainy-Day Savings Account** with a desired initial amount of money deposited into it. That money is withdrawn from the **Primary Savings Account**. Then the "pay yourself *last*, but always pay yourself *something*" process can begin. Once initiated and done for a few months, it begins to become a routine task. You look at your checking account balance for the end of the prior month, split it into halves and deposit those into the two savings accounts. Continue to practice it faithfully and develop discipline in doing it.

Because each month's bills, credit card purchases, and other expenses paid by cash or check vary, the **EOM** amount differs from month to month. On some occasions, I notice that my next needed check will overdraw my checking account and, if done, the **EOM** is projected to be negative. To cover the shortage, I take the needed amount of money from my **Rainy-Day Savings Account**. After my paycheck for the end of that month is deposited, I pay back the borrowed amount by depositing the borrowed amount into **Rainy-Day Savings Account**.

As an example, for an anticipated shortage of $60 I

transfer $60 from my **Rainy-Day Savings Account** into my checking account. That makes the **EOM** amount $0. Once my next paycheck is deposited into my checking account, I transfer $60 from it into my **Rainy-Day Savings Account**.

Over the long-term, my play book continues like this. When the balance in the **Primary Savings Account** reaches the target balance, I will have a solid feeling of financial security. Now I can allocate its subsequent **½ EOM** amounts to specific short- and long-term needs. Examples include saving money for my child's college costs, a future car purchase, my daughter's future wedding, a down payment on a first home, investments, retirement planning, funeral costs etc.

Avoiding comingling money helps one to be disciplined about accumulating funds needed for each future need. As such needs come about, create a separate savings account for each one. Then deposit the subsequent **½ EOM** funds into the separate savings accounts either equally or in differing allocations. As the funds build up, I periodically move some funds into certificates of deposit accounts to earn greater interest. When the balance in the **Rainy-**

Day Savings Account rises sufficiently above the target minimum balance, it allows me the choice to do "smell the roses" types of activities. It will happen frequently enough to sustain a happy outlook on life.

With diligent management of an accurate personal **budget** the balances in both savings accounts will steadily rise. So, let's turn to the process of creating and using a household budget.

LESSON 4

Budgets and Budget Busters

"Life in the city can make you crazy for sounds of the sand and the sea.
Life in a high-rise can make you hungry for things that you can't even see.
Fly away, fly away, fly away."

These lyrics from John Denver's song "Fly Away!" express the urges we all feel to get away from life's daily routine. To do so often enough, most of us must be patient and save money religiously. Keeping expenditures consistent with an accurate budget accomplishes that. Unfortunately, a lot of people procrastinate in developing the accurate budget needed to do that. Because it takes work, lots of people treat it like a birthday wish. They blow out the budget candles, but the wish never materializes.

In businesses, schools, and other organizations, budgeting is essential to being successful. Successful entities do budget and they do it well. Establishing allocations and a bottom line for expenditures are key to sustaining their monetary capital. The impetus to "keep to our bottom line" closely hovers over every good owner and financial officer. Somehow, for lots of people and households that necessity and commitment do not carry over to developing and using a personal or family budget. Why so?

Budgeting does not make it onto many people's list of exciting things they need TO DO. There is lots of enthusiasm for researching and preparing to bet on the Kentucky Derby. And it is fun to plan for and to land in Hawaii for a sunny vacation. Preparing a budget does not come close to providing such joys.

More so, budgeting brings on the need to track one's spending and faithfully record it monthly. Realistically, it can be like maintaining a planned daily exercise routine. It is not easy to keep doing it every day. Some days it happens. Other days it does not. Quite often the latter begins to dominate and eventually the exercising ceases. Every year I see that happen at my health club.

January brings a surge of determined new members; buoyed by a New Year's resolution to finally begin to lose weight. Then the challenge of maintaining self-motivation begins to set in and increase. By March many of the newbies have departed; their dedication and commitment having petered out. Typically, it is the lack of a routine process and an encouraging buddy that wears down the individual. For some who stay, they turn to formal group classes and/or a personal trainer I have been down that path myself. CrossFit workouts became my choice. Now 7+ years later, the coaching and camaraderie it offers keeps me going.

Similarly, lots of people resolve to begin household budgeting at the start of the coming New Year. They too begin energetically. But they also can fall prey to diminishing self-motivation. If the effort becomes lackadaisical or lack of commitment creeps in, then budgeting becomes a hit or miss process. Some months it happens. Other months it does not. And that will not work. Utilizing a household budget requires a routine process and attentiveness to it.

Are you a person who just never gets around to preparing a budget for your income? If so, then you are not alone. And if two people are involved, then creating and using a mutual budget can be prone to contention, even angry disagreements. With a proper approach to the task, you can develop a personal budget gradually over time. If there are two of you doing it, you can minimize or avoid stress over competing needs and perspective as well. Subsequently, I will be showing and explaining how to accomplish both. For now, let's just look at the make-up of an effective budget format.

A **budget** is a tabulated plan specifying how some amount of money will be allocated or spent during a period of time. For household budgeting that amount of money is typically the **MONTHLY** take-home pay (**MONTHLY** gross pay minus withholdings for taxes etc.). The period for expending it is a month. The amount of money can also be the **ANNUAL** take-home pay (**ANNUAL** gross pay minus withholdings for taxes etc.) and the period is a year. Ideally, both **MONTHLY** and **ANNUAL** budgets are used.

Without a budget in place, spending money becomes an aimless, haphazard activity. Such spending leads to buying unnecessary things. Some things are bought simply because you either want to have it (e.g., a wine cooling refrigerator) or to do it (e.g., a golfing excursion). That is called impulsive spending. You act despite not knowing if the purchase is affordable within your income.

Credit card usage is so readily available for one to access that it is the main nemesis for making impulsive, frivolous purchases. An impulsive, frivolous purchase is something you buy that sooner or later you regret having bought. What those specifically might be will differ for each reader.

Frivolous or not, impulsive purchases are budget busters. Regret surfaces when you read the outstanding balance on your credit card statement and then feel surprised, shocked, or even stunned by the amount due. You realize you let the credit card burn a hole in your pocket. You scan the individual entries and find a couple high-cost impulsive purchases and many smaller impulsive purchases have led to that surprise setback.

You forgot you bought that small portable television for when you go camping but only go camping once per year at best. You forgot you bought a brand-new driver and/or putter sure to improve your golf game, which you play twice per year. Gosh you dined out at "affordable places" eight times and collectively spent $600.00, not including tips. You rented some movies to save the $20.00 cost of going to the movie theater once, but you spent $60.00 on the rentals. You have eight pairs of shoes but just had to have those cute blue ones that match an outfit you have but only wear "occasionally". Oh yes, you had the guys over to watch the BIG GAME and, oops, you spent $100.00 on food and beer.

We all do such things now and then. The key is the "now and then" part. Not all of us do it only now and then.

People who are frivolous "only now and then" and plan for (save for) the expenses greatly enhance their ability to consistently save money and accumulate more and more savings over time. Those savings allow them to worry less about paying ongoing necessary bills and surprise bills. They can enjoy life. Otherwise, frivolous overspending creeps in and can become a habit. You do not have an organized record of how your money is being spent and how much of it is being spent in total. Preparing a budget and following it overcomes that. So, let's discuss budgeting.

NOTE: The author assumes you do not have a budget in place. In that context, the following overview provides a solid start on a path to develop an effective beginner's budget. If you do have a budget in place, then the overview offers a path to improve it.

Creating a budget table

A budget table is a compilation of and comparison of two things for a given period of time: 1) the amount of money from your take-home pay that you anticipate spending on each of various Budget Categories, and 2) the amounts of money you spend on each Budget Category. For 1), the amounts are termed **Allocations**. For 2) the amounts are termed **Amounts Spent**. The period is either **MONTHLY** or **ANNUALLY**.

All expenses fall into two types: **fixed expenses** (necessary things which are fixed in amount, such as rent) and **variable expenses** (necessary things which change in amount, such as groceries). Variable expenses also include discretionary expenses (optional things one can live without, such as tickets to a concert or travel costs).

In a budget table you list all the Budget Categories in which you plan to spend your take-home pay. You group them into the two types of expenses, i.e., fixed, and variable.

Next to each Budget Category, you list the amount in dollars from your **ANNUAL** take-home pay that you allocate to it (the **ANNUAL Allocation**). The sum of these allocations must equal your **ANNUAL** take-home pay.

As conflicting as it sounds, in a budget, saving money is an expense. And it is the most challenging expense to afford. Include a fixed Budget Category Regular Savings for money you intend to deposit in your Primary Savings Account every month. Include a variable Budget Category 1/2 EOM to Primary Savings for possible additional money to be deposited into that account at the end of the month. Include a Budget Category 1/2 EOM to Rainy-Day Savings for possible money to be deposited into your Rainy-Day Savings Account.

Dividing each **ANNUAL Allocation** by 12 produces the corresponding **MONTHLY Allocation** (**MONTHLY** budgeted amount). The total of these allocations must equal your **MONTHLY** take-home pay.

After the end of the month, next to each Budget Category, you list the **Amount Spent** on it that month. Wait until your monthly checking account and credit card (and/or debit card) statements are available with that information.

The sum **(*OVERALL TOTAL*)** of the **Amounts Spent** is to be compared with your **MONTHLY** take-home pay. If the ***OVERALL TOTAL*** is equal to your **MONTHLY** take-home pay, then you have "matched" your budget. If it is less than your **MONTHLY** take-home pay, then you have "underspent" (or "met") your budget. If it is more than the **MONTHLY** take-home pay, then you have "overspent" (or "not met") your budget.

<u>Numerical Examples</u>

<u>Example 1</u>

The following is a simplified example of a personal budget. It is based on an **ANNUAL** take-home pay of $34000. For ease initially, the Budget Categories are limited and identified simply as Categories 1-9. One of them is for Regular Savings. In addition, Budget Categories are included for the ½ EOM to Primary Savings and ½ EOM to Rainy-Day Savings money.

TABLE 1

1	2	3	4	5
2020 BUDGET CATEGORIES	ANNUAL Allocation	MONTHLY Allocation	Amount Spent	MONTHLY Allocation - Amount Spent
FIXED				
1	480	40	40	0
2	2400	200	200	0
3	300	25	25	0
4	12000	1000	1000	0
VARIABLE				
5	3000	250	200	50
6	580	48	135	-87
7	360	30	0	30
8	480	40	138	-98
9	12000	1000	719	281
SUB-TOTAL	31600	2633	2457	176
½ EOM to	1200	100	188	-88

Primary Savings				
½ EOM to Rainy-Day Savings	**1200**	**100**	**188**	**-88**
OVERALL TOTAL	***34000***	***2833***	***2833***	***0***

Column 1 lists the Budget Categories. They are separated into four fixed Budget Categories, five variable Budget Categories and the two variable ½ EOM Budget Categories. **Column 2** contains the **ANNUAL Allocation** (amount budgeted) for each Budget Category. For example, Budget Category 6 is allocated \$580 and each 1/2 EOM Category is allocated \$1200. The **ANNUAL Allocations** for Budget Categories 1 through 9 **SUB-TOTAL** \$31600. Adding in the two ½ EOM **ANNUAL Allocations**, the ***OVERALL TOTAL*** of the **ANNUAL Allocations** is \$34000.

Then dividing each of the **ANNUAL Allocations** by 12 provides the **MONTHLY Allocations** listed in **column 3**. For example, Budget Category 6 has a **MONTHLY Allocation** of \$580/12 = \$48 (rounded). Summing them gives \$2833.

NOTE: The ***OVERALL TOTAL*** should be, and is, equal to $34000 by 12 = $2833 (rounded).

The **Amount Spent** in each Budget Category during that month are listed in **column 4**. For example, $200 was spent on the fixed Budget Category 2 and $135 was spent on the variable Budget Category 6.

The **Amount Spent** for the ½ EOM to Primary Savings and the ½ EOM to Rainy-Day Savings is half the amount left over after all other **Amounts Spent** are subtracted from the **MONTHLY** take-home pay of $2833. In this example, the amount left over = EOM = $2833 - $2457 = $376. Thus, ½ EOM = $376/2 = $188. That is the amount deposited into each of the savings accounts at the end of the month.

The amounts listed in **column 5** for each Budget Category were calculated by subtracting the **Amount Spent** from the corresponding **MONTHLY Allocation**. A positive result indicates the **MONTHLY Allocation** was underspent. A negative result indicates it was overspent. For example, Budget Category 5 was underspent by $250 - $200 = $50 and Budget Category 6 was overspent by $48 - $135 = –$87. Each

½ EOM Budget Category was overspent by $100 – $188 = –$88.

NOTE: For the ½ EOM Budget Categories, the negative amount is a positive outcome. It indicates you were able to put $88 more into each account than anticipated.

NOTE: The ***OVERALL TOTAL*** of **column 5** is $0. That is because the ***OVERALL TOTAL*** for the **MONTHLY Allocations** and for the **Amounts Spent** are the same, namely $2833. That is as it should be. The two **½** EOM expenditures cause that to happen and it will always be the case.

Using the above results, **Adjusted MONTHLY Allocations** can be obtained. That is done by changing the prior **MONTHLY Allocations** to reflect the actual **Amounts Spent**.

If a Budget Category was overspent, then its allocation is <u>increased</u> by the amount it was overspent. If a Budget Category is underspent, then its allocation is <u>reduced</u> by the amount that it was underspent. These adjustments are illustrated in the following table.

TABLE 2

1	2	3	4	5	6
2020 BUDGET CATEGORIES	ANNUAL Allocation	MONTHLY Allocation	Amount Spent	MONTHLY Allocation - Amount Spent	Adjusted MONTHLY Allocation
FIXED					
1	480	40	40	0	40
2	2400	200	200	0	200
3	300	25	25	0	25
4	12000	1000	1000	0	1000
VARIABLE					
5	3000	250	200	50	200
6	580	48	135	–87	135
7	360	30	0	30	0
8	480	40	138	–98	138
9	12000	1000	719	281	719
SUB-TOTAL	31600	2633	2457	176	2457
½ EOM to Primary Savings	1200	100	188	–88	188
½ EOM to Rainy-Day Savings	1200	100	188	–88	188
OVERALL TOTAL	*34000*	*2833*	*2833*	*0*	*2833*

Column 6, with the heading **Adjusted MONTHLY Allocation**, has been added to Table 1. The **Adjusted MONTHLY Allocation** amounts are obtained by subtracting the amount listed in **column 5** from the corresponding **MONTHLY Allocation** listed in **column 3**.

For example, for Budget Category 5 the value listed in **column 5** is $250 – $200 = $50. Because Budget Category 5 was <u>underspent</u> by $50, the **MONTHLY Allocation** is to be reduced by that amount. The **Adjusted MONTHLY Allocation** is $250 – $50 = $200.

In contrast, for Budget Category 6 the value listed in **column 5** is $48 – ($135) = –$87. Because Budget Category 6 was <u>overspent</u> by $87, the **MONTHLY Allocation** is to be increased by that amount. The **Adjusted MONTHLY Allocation** is $48 – (– $87) = $135.

For each savings account ½ EOM Budget Category, the **Adjusted MONTHLY Allocation** is $100 – (–$88) = $188. That is an increase because you were able to put an extra $88 into each of them.

In general, Budget Categories that were overspent in the prior month required more money. Each **MONTHLY Allocation** is increased by that additional amount. Budget Categories that were underspent in the prior month required less money. Each **MONTHLY Allocation** is decreased by the difference in amount. The **Adjusted MONTHLY Allocation** for the ½ EOM Budget Categories balance the budget to the ***OVERALL TOTAL*** of $2833. The **Adjusted MONTHLY Allocations** could be used as the **MONTHLY Allocations** for the following month.

NOTE: Observe that each **Adjusted MONTHLY Allocation** and the corresponding **Amount Spent** are the same amount. In other words, the **Amounts Spent** could be used as the **MONTHLY Allocations** for the next month.

Example 2

Table 2 is repeated below, with one difference. The **Amount Spent** on Budget Category 9 has been changed from $719 to $1023. That's an increase of $304.

TABLE 3

1	2	3	4	5	6
2020 BUDGET CATEGORIES	ANNUAL Allocation	MONTHLY Allocation	Amount Spent	MONTHLY Allocation – Amount Spent	Adjusted MONTHLY Allocation
FIXED					
1	480	40	40	0	40
2	2400	200	200	0	200
3	300	25	25	0	25
4	12000	1000	1000	0	1000
VARIABLE					
5	250	250	200	50	200
6	580	48	135	-87	135
7	360	30	0	30	0
8	480	40	138	-98	138
9	12000	1000	1023	-23	1023
SUB-TOTAL	**31600**	**2633**	**2761**	**-128**	**2761**
1/2 EOM to Primary Savings	1200	100	36	64	36
1/2 EOM to Rainy-Day Savings	1200	100	36	64	36
OVERALL TOTAL	***34000***	***2833***	***2833***	***0***	***2833***

In **column 4**, the new **SUB-TOTAL** is $2761. Consequently, EOM = $2833 – $2761 = $72 and the **Amount Spent** for ½ EOM to Primary Savings and the 1/2 EOM to Rainy-Day Savings is ½ EOM = $72/2 = $36. That is the amount to be deposited into each of those savings accounts at the end of the month. In contrast to Example 1, the amount is less than the allocated $100.

As before, the values in **column 5** are the **MONTHLY Allocation – Amount Spent** for each Budget Category. The result listed for Budget Category 9 has changed. Previously it was <u>underspent</u> by $281. In this case, the result is $1000 – $1023 = –$23. The negative value indicates Budget Category 9 is <u>overspent</u> by $23. The **Adjusted MONTHLY Allocation** is increased to $1000 + $23 = $1023.

In this example, the **SUB-TOTAL** for **column 5** Is -$128 Indicating It Is <u>overspent</u>. For each savings account, the result In **column 5** Is $64. That's because each was <u>underspent</u> by $100 – $36 = $64, a total of $128. That amount offsets the overspent **SUB-TOTAL**. Hence the ***OVERALL TOTAL*** of $0.

In column 6, the **Adjusted MONTHLY Allocation** is reduced to \$100 – \$64 = \$36. That's because you were able to put only \$36 into them, not the initial **MONTHLY Allocation** of \$100.

Example 3

Table 3 is repeated below, with one difference. The **Amount Spent** on Budget Category 9 has been changed from \$1023 to \$1225, an increase of \$202.

TABLE 4

1	2	3	4	5	6	7
2020 BUDGET CATEGORIES	ANNUAL Allocation	MONTHLY Allocation	Amount Spent	MONTHLY Allocation – Amount Spent	Adjusted MONTHLY Allocation	2nd Adjusted MONTHLY Allocation
FIXED						
1	480	40	40	0	40	40
2	2400	200	200	0	200	200
3	300	25	25	0	25	25
4	12000	1000	1000	0	1000	1000
VARIABLE						
5	3000	250	200	50	200	200
6	580	48	135	-87	135	135
7	360	30	0	30	0	0
8	480	40	138	-98	138	138

9	12000	1000	1225	-225	1225	1095
SUB-TOTAL	31600	2633	2963	-330	2963	2833
½ EOM to Primary Savings	1200	100	-65	165	-65	0
½ EOM to Rainy-Day Savings	1200	100	-65	165	-65	0
OVERALL TOTAL	*34000*	*2833*	*2833*	*0*	*2833*	*2833*

In this example, the **SUB-TOTAL** of the **Amounts Spent** is \$2963. That exceeds the ***OVERALL TOTAL*** of the **MONTHLY Allocations** by \$2963 – \$2833 = \$130. In other words, EOM = \$2833 – \$2983 = –\$130. Consequently, there is no EOM money available to put into the savings accounts.

To cover that shortage, you take \$65 from each of the savings accounts. Because you took money out of instead of putting money into those accounts the ½ EOM = –\$65. That amount is entered as the **Amount Spent** on each 1/2 EOM Budget Category. That balances the budget at the ***OVERALL TOTAL*** of \$2833.

The values in **column 5** are the **MONTHLY Allocation – Amount Spent** for each Budget Category. The result listed for Budget Category 9 has changed. Previously it was underspent by \$23. In this case, it is overspent by \$225. Consequently, the **Adjusted MONTHLY Allocation** is increased to \$1000 + \$225 = \$1225.

The **SUB-TOTAL** for **column 5** is -\$330. It is overspent. For each ½ EOM Budget Category, the result in **column 5** is \$165. That's because each was underspent by \$100 - (-\$65) = \$165, a total of \$330. That amount offsets the overspent **SUB-TOTAL.** Hence the ***OVERALL TOTAL*** of \$0.

It might seem odd that each savings account was underspent, but that result is correct! The **MONTHLY Allocation** was to put \$100 into each of them. Instead, you had to take \$65 out of each of them. In total, you put \$165 less into each of them than the **MONTHLY Allocation** of \$100, the \$100 you did not put in plus the \$65 you took out.

The resulting **Adjusted MONTHLY Allocation** for each savings account is –\$65, an amount that is not possible. That outcome necessitates a **2nd Adjusted**

MONTHLY Allocation as listed in **column 7**. Only two changes have been made.

For each savings account, the **Adjusted MONTHLY Allocation** was increased from –$65 to $0. To offset that change the **Adjusted MONTHLY Allocation** for Budget Category 9 was decreased by $130, from $1225 to $1095. That is done to maintain the ***OVERALL TOTAL*** of the **2nd Adjusted MONTHLY Allocations** at $2833.

Again, the **Adjusted MONTHLY Allocations** amounts are the same as the **Amounts Spent**. You could use the listed **Amounts Spent** as the **MONTHLY Allocations** for the following month.

Example 4

There are other alternatives for handling the **Adjusted MONTHLY Allocation** of –$65 that resulted for the saving accounts in Example 3. In that example, the **2nd Adjusted MONTHLY Allocation** for each ½ EOM Budget Category was $0. In other words, you anticipate not putting any EOM money into them.

What if, instead, you want to put be able to put $100 (the original **MONTHLY Allocation**) into each of them next month? You can do that by reducing the **MONTHLY Allocation** for Budget Category 9 by more than $130. Here is how you make the adjustment.

To accommodate the desired **2nd MONTHLY Allocation** of $100 for each savings account, you offset those increases by reducing the **Adjusted MONTHLY Allocation** for Budget Category 9 from the $1095 In Example 4 to $895, $200 less.

Then, to maintain the ***OVERALL TOTAL*** of $2833 for the **2nd Adjusted MONTHLY Allocation** for each ½ EOM Budget Category is set at $100. The following table shows the adjusted portion of the Table 4. The dashed lines represent the omitted lines. Only the entries in **column 7** are different from those contained in Table 4.

TABLE 5

1	2	3	4	5	6	7
2020 BUDGET CATEGORIES	ANNUAL Allocation	MONTHLY Allocation	Amount Spent	MONTHLY Allocation – Amount Spent	Adjusted MONTHLY Allocation	2nd Adjusted MONTHLY Allocation

9	12000	1000	1225	-225	1225	895
SUB-TOTAL	*31600*	*2633*	*2963*	*-330*	*2963*	*2633*
½ EOM to Primary Savings	1200	100	-65	165	-65	100
½ EOM to Rainy-Day Savings	1200	100	-65	165	-65	100
OVERALL TOTAL	*34000*	*2833*	*2833*	*0*	*2833*	*2833*

Example 5

Another alternative to Example 4 is to take the entire $130 shortage out of the Rainy-Day Savings Account.

TABLE 6

1	2	3	4	5	6	7
2020 BUDGET CATEGORIES	ANNUAL Allocation	MONTHLY Allocation	Amount Spent	MONTHLY Allocation – Amount Spent	Adjusted MONTHLY Allocation	2nd Adjusted MONTHLY Allocation
9	12000	1000	1225	-225	1225	895
SUB-TOTAL	31600	2633	2963	-330	2963	2633
½ EOM to Primary Savings	1200	100	0	100	0	100

½ EOM to Rainy-Day Savings	**1200**	**100**	**-130**	**230**	**-130**	**100**
OVERALL TOTAL	***34000***	***2833***	***2833***	***0***	***2833***	***2833***

In **column 4**, the **Amount Spent** on 1/2 EOM to Primary Savings has been changed from –$65 to $0. The result (in **column 5**) is that the Budget Category is underspent by $100. Subtracting that amount from the **MONTHLY Allocation** gives (in **column 6**) the **Adjusted MONTHLY Allocation** of $0.

Also, in **column 4**, the **Amount Spent** on 1/2 EOM to Rainy-Day Savings has been changed from –$65 to –$130. The result (in **column 5**) is the **Budget Category** is underspent by $230. Subtracting that amount from the **MONTHLY Allocation** gives the **Adjusted MONTHLY Allocation** of $100 – $230 = –$130, as listed in **column 6**. This necessitates a second adjustment.

The **2nd Adjusted MONTHLY Allocations** are listed in **column 7**. As in Example 4, the choice made was to set the **2nd Adjusted MONTHLY Allocation** for the Primary Savings Account and the Rainy-Day Savings Account to the initial amount of $100 each. To offset and keep the ***OVERALL TOTAL*** at $2833, the **Adjusted MONTHLY Allocation** for Budget Category 9 is reduced by $200, from $1095 to $895.

NOTE: The **2nd Adjusted MONTHLY Allocations** are the same amounts as In Example 4 (Table 5). That's expected, as the only difference Is how the overspent $130 in **column 4** was handled in 1/2 EOM amounts for the two savings accounts. In Example 4, $65 of the $130 shortage was taken from each of them. In Example 5, the entire $130 shortage was taken from the Rainy-Day Savings account.

NOTE: In the above examples. the use of Budget Category 9 in the adjusted MONTHLY Allocations was arbitrary. Other choices could be made.

LESSON 5

Application to Realistic Budgets

The examples in Lesson 4 illustrate the technique of creating a budget table. For simplification, there were only nine generic Budget Categories plus the two ½ EOM Budget Categories. Real budgets involve many more Budget Categories. Although the technique is the same, the budget tables become more involved.

Example 6

The following is a hypothetical, but realistic, budget based upon a young individual who rents a residence and has an **ANNUAL** take-home pay of $47000. Because the vertical length of the table extends for three pages, for ease of reading, the column headings are repeated at the bottom of the table.

TABLE 7

1	2	3	4	5	6
2020 BUDGET CATEGORIES	ANNUAL Allocation	MONTHLY Allocation	Amount Spent	MONTHLY Allocation - Amount Spent	Adjusted MONTHLY Allocation
FIXED					

Cable TV	**450**	**38**	**38**	**0**	**38**
Insurance-Auto	**600**	**50**	**50**	**0**	**50**
Insurance-Medical	**3800**	**317**	**317**	**0**	**317**
Insurance-Dental	**420**	**35**	**35**	**0**	**35**
Insurance-Life	**360**	**30**	**30**	**0**	**30**
Internet	**250**	**21**	**21**	**0**	**21**
Regular Savings	**600**	**50**	**50**	**0**	**50**
Rent	**13400**	**1117**	**1117**	**0**	**1117**
Cell Phone Service	**600**	**50**	**50**	**0**	**50**
VARIABLE					
Auto Fuel + Maintenance	**3000**	**250**	**321**	**-71**	**321**
Clothing	**600**	**50**	**0**	**50**	**0**
Computer Supplies	**400**	**33**	**30**	**3**	**30**
Dental	**450**	**38**	**0**	**38**	**0**
Dining and Entertainment	**3200**	**267**	**234**	**33**	**234**
Eye Care	**500**	**42**	**0**	**42**	**0**
Gifts	**600**	**50**	**0**	**50**	**0**
Groceries	**3200**	**267**	**322**	**-55**	**322**
Home Maintenance and Repairs	**500**	**42**	**0**	**42**	**0**
Household	**600**	**50**	**77**	**-27**	**77**

Laundry/Dry Cleaning	**150**	**13**	**15**	**-2**	**15**
Liquor	**600**	**50**	**66**	**-16**	**66**
Medical	**1200**	**100**	**0**	**100**	**0**
Personal Care	**800**	**67**	**77**	**-10**	**77**
Postage	**60**	**5**	**12**	**-7**	**12**
Trash Service	**387**	**32**	**32**	**0**	**32**
Travel	**1500**	**125**	**0**	**125**	**0**
Utilities	**2800**	**231**	**344**	**-113**	**344**
Miscellaneous	**1173**	**98**	**144**	**-46**	**144**
SUB-TOTAL	**42200**	**3517**	**3381**	**136**	**3381**
½ EOM to Primary Savings	**2400**	**200**	**268**	**-68**	**268**
½ EOM to Rainy-Day Savings	**2400**	**200**	**268**	**-68**	**268**
OVERALL TOTAL	***47000***	***3917***	***3917***	***0***	***3917***
2020 BUDGET CATEGORIES	ANNUAL Allocation	MONTHLY Allocation	Amount Spent	MONTHLY Allocation - Amount Spent	Adjusted MONTHLY Allocation
1	2	3	4	5	6

Column 1 lists the Budget Categories alphabetically and separated into fixed expenses and variable expenses. The fixed expenses include a Budget

Category for Regular Savings. It is for the fixed amount of money you intend to put into your Primary Savings Account when you get your paycheck at the beginning of each month. Budget Categories are included for the variable ½ EOM amount of money you anticipate putting into each savings account.

Column 2 lists the **ANNUAL Allocation** for each Budget Category. They are reasonable amounts for such an income level. The **SUB-TOTAL** is the sum of the listed **ANNUAL Allocation**s, excluding the two ½ EOM Budget Categories. In this case, the **SUB-TOTAL** is $42200. That leaves an EOM = $47000 – $42200 = $4800, thus a ½ EOM = $2400. The ***OVERALL TOTAL*** of the **ANNUAL Allocations** is $47000. As it should be, the amount is equal to the **ANNUAL** take-home pay.

Dividing each **ANNUAL Allocation** by 12 gives the **MONTHLY Allocations** listed in **column 3**. The ***OVERALL TOTAL*** of them is $3917. As it should be, the amount is equal to $47000 by 12 = $3917 (rounded).

The **Amounts Spent** in each Budget Category for January are listed in **column 4**. In this case, the **SUB-TOTAL** = $3381. Amounts listed for the ½ EOM to Primary Savings and the ½ EOM to Rainy-Day Savings are half the amount left over after all other expenditures are subtracted from the **MONTHLY** take-home pay of $3917. In this case, the amount left over = EOM = $3917 – $3381 = $536 and ½ EOM = $536/2 = $268. That amount that would be deposited into each savings account at the end of the month.

As done before, the values in **column 5** were calculated for each Budget Category by subtracting the **Amount Spent** from the **MONTHLY Allocation.** For example, Computer Supplies were <u>underspent</u> by $33 – $30 = $3 and Groceries were <u>overspent</u> by $267 – $322 = –$55. Each ½ EOM Budget Category comes out as <u>overspent</u> by $200 – $268 = –$68. As expected, the ***OVERALL TOTAL*** for **column 5** is $0.

Column 6 lists the **Adjusted MONTHLY Allocations**. For example, for Dining + Entertainment, the result is $267 – $33 = $234. Because the Budget Category was <u>underspent</u> by $33, the **MONTHLY Allocation** has been decreased to $234. In contrast, for Personal Care, the result is $67 – (–$10) = $67 + $10 = $77. Because the Budget Category was <u>overspent</u> by $10, the **MONTHLY Allocation** has been increased to $77.

Also, for each ½ EOM Budget Category, the result is \$200 – (–\$68) = \$268. Because you were able to put that higher amount into each of them, each **MONTHLY Allocation** has been increased to \$268.

NOTE: The Clothing, Dental, Eye Care, Home Repair and Maintenance, and Travel categories each have an **Adjusted MONTHLY Allocation** of \$0.

Example 7

In Example 6, the **SUB-TOTAL** of the **Amounts Spent** was less than the **MONTHLY** take-home pay. Let's look at an example of that **SUB-TOTAL** being more than the **MONTHLY** take-home pay.

TABLE 8

1	2	3	4	5	6	7
2020 BUDGET CATEGORIES	ANNUAL Allocation	MONTHLY Allocation	Amount Spent	MONTHLY Allocation – Amount Spent	Adjusted MONTHLY Allocation	2nd Adjusted MONTHLY Allocation
FIXED						
Cable TV	450	38	38	0	38	38
Insurance-Auto	600	50	50	0	50	50
Insurance-Medical	3800	317	317	0	317	317

Insurance-Dental	420	35	35	0	35	35
Insurance-Life	360	30	30	0	30	30
Internet	250	21	21	0	21	21
Regular Savings	600	50	50	0	50	50
Rent	13400	1117	1117	0	1117	1117
Trash Service	387	32	32	0	32	32
Cell Phone Service	600	50	50	0	50	50
VARIABLE						
Auto Fuel + Maintenance	3000	250	356	-106	356	356
Clothing	600	50	135	-85	135	135
Computer Supplies	400	33	0	33	0	0
Dental	450	38	240	-202	240	240
Dining and Entertainment	3200	267	276	-9	276	276
Eye Care	500	42	0	42	0	0
Gifts	600	50	75	-25	75	75
Groceries	3200	267	350	-83	350	350
Home Maintenance and Repairs	500	42	54	-12	54	54
Household	600	50	90	-40	90	90
Laundry/Dry Cleaning	150	13	0	13	0	0
Liquor	600	50	75	-25	75	75
Medical	1200	100	0	100	0	0
Personal Care	800	67	77	-10	77	77
Postage	60	5	22	-17	22	22

Trash Service	**387**	**32**	**32**	**0**	**32**	**32**
Travel	**1500**	**125**	**0**	**125**	**0**	**0**
Utilities	**2800**	**231**	**344**	**-113**	**344**	**344**
Misc.	**1173**	**98**	**144**	**-46**	**144**	**84**
SUB-TOTAL	**42200**	**3517**	**3977**	**-460**	**3917**	**3917**
½ EOM to Primary Savings	**2400**	**200**	**-30**	**230**	**-30**	**0**
½ EOM to Rainy-Day Savings	**2400**	**200**	**-30**	**230**	**-30**	**0**
OVERALL TOTAL	***47000***	***3917***	***3917***	***0***	***3917***	***3917***
2020 BUDGET CATEGORIES	ANNUAL Allocation	MONTHLY Allocation	Amount Spent	MONTHLY Allocation – Amount Spent	Adjusted MONTHLY Allocation	2nd Adjusted MONTHLY Allocation
1	2	3	4	5	6	7

The **MONTHLY Allocations** to each Budget Category are the same as in Table 7, but the **Amounts Spent** on some of the variable Budget Categories have been changed. Let's walk through the effects.

The **SUB-TOTAL** of the **Amounts Spent** is \$3977, which exceeds the ***OVERALL TOTAL*** of the **MONTHLY Allocations** by \$3917 – \$3977 = –\$60. As a result, there is no EOM money available to put into the savings accounts. To cover that shortage, you take

$30 from each of the savings accounts. Because you took money out instead of putting money into those accounts the **Amount Spent** on each ½ EOM Budget Category is –$30. That balances the budget at $3917.

The **Adjusted MONTHLY Allocations** are calculated as done previously. As before, the **Adjusted MONTHLY Allocations** are the same as the **Amounts Spent**.

NOTE: The **Adjusted MONTHLY Allocations** for Computer Supplies, Eye Care, Laundry/Dry Cleaning, and Medical are all $0.

The **Adjusted MONTHLY Allocations** to each 1/2 EOM Budget Category is –$30. an amount which is not possible. That necessitates a **2nd Adjusted MONTHLY Budget** as listed in **column 7**. Only two changes have been made. The 1/2 EOM amount for each savings account is changed to $0. To offset that change, the amount of the **Adjusted MONTHLY Allocation** for Miscellaneous is reduced by $60, namely from $144 to $84. That balances the budget at $3917.

The adjustments made to the **MONTHLY Allocations** lead to the noted oddities. Moreover, the **Amounts**

Spent on the variable expenses will be different each month. How do you handle these aspects in succeeding months? Let's look at my approach to it.

LESSON 6

Creating an Accurate Monthly Budget – On the fly!

Your budgeting flight has just taken off. You have taken the steps of creating your budget table and tracking your spending for one month.

You could use the resulting **Adjusted MONTHLY Allocations** for the next month. However, as seen above, using a single month to get **Adjusted MONTHLY Allocations** is insufficient. By doing that, some Budget Categories result in $0 allocated to them. More importantly, it was observed that the **Adjusted MONTHLY Allocations** were the same as the **Amounts Spent**. However, your variable expenses will change every month. Some fixed expenses might be billed quarterly or annually.

To account for the changing **MONTHLY Amounts Spent**, you need to use the <u>average</u> **MONTHLY Amounts Spent** that occur over a period time. Ideally, that would be a year. Well, waiting a year is a long time. Instead, the **Adjusted MONTHLY Allocations** can be developed gradually, on a month-to-month basis.

Example 8

Assume you make no adjustment to the **MONTHLY Allocations** used in January and repeat the tracking process in February. The following is the expanded budget table.

TABLE 9

1	2	3	4	5	6	7	8
2020 BUDGET CATEGORIES	ANNUAL Allocation	MONTHLY Allocation	# of MONTHS	Amount Spent			Avg. Amount Spent
			2	Jan.	Feb.	Jan-Feb	
FIXED							
Cable TV	450	38	76	38	38	76	38
Insurance - Auto	600	50	100	50	50	100	50
Insurance-Medical	3800	317	634	317	317	634	317
Insurance-Dental	420	35	70	35	35	70	35
Insurance-Life	360	30	60	30	30	60	30
Internet	250	21	42	21	21	42	21
Reg. Savings	600	50	100	50	50	100	50
Rent	13400	1117	2234	1117	1117	2234	1117

Cell Phone Service	*600*	50	100	50	50	100	50
VARIABLE							
Auto Fuel + Maintenance	3000	250	500	321	277	598	299
Clothing	600	50	100	0	52	52	26
Computer Supplies	400	33	66	30	0	30	15
Dental	450	38	76	0	0	0	0
Dining + Entertain.	3200	267	534	234	265	499	250
Eye Care	500	42	84	0	350	350	175
Gifts	600	50	100	0	0	0	0
Groceries	3200	267	534	322	255	577	288
Home Maintenance and Repairs	500	42	84	0	23	23	12
Household	600	50	100	77	55	132	66
Laundry/Dry Cleaning	150	13	26	15	0	15	8
Liquor	600	50	100	66	88	154	77
Medical	1200	100	200	0	65	65	32
Personal Care	800	67	134	77	63	140	70
Postage	60	5	10	12	4	16	8
Trash Service	387	32	64	32	0	32	16
Travel	1500	125	250	0	0	0	0
Utilities	2800	231	462	344	301	645	322
Misc.	1173	98	196	144	56	200	100
SUB -TOTAL	42200	3517	7034	3381	3561	6942	3471
½ EOM to Primary Savings	2400	200	400	268	178	446	223

½ EOM to Rainy-Day Savings	2400	200	400	268	178	446	223
OVERALL TOTAL	*47000*	*3917*	*7834*	*3917*	*3917*	*7834*	*3917*
2020 BUDGET CATEGORIES	ANNUAL Allocation	MONTHLY Allocation	2 # of MONTHS	Jan. Amount Spent	Feb.	Jan-Feb	Avg. Amount Spent
1	2	3	4	5	6	7	8

Columns 1-3 are identical to those in Table 7. **Column 4** indicates this budget table is for a two-month period. Multiplying the **MONTHLY Allocations** in **column 3** by 2 gives the values listed in **column 4**. The **Amounts Spent** in January and February are listed in **columns 5 and 6**. Those for January are the same as in Table 7.

Amounts Spent listed in **column 7** are obtained by combining the individual **Amounts Spent** in **columns 5 and 6**. Dividing each amount by 2 gives the **Average Amounts Spent** for the two-month period. Results are listed in **column 8**. For example, the **Amount Spent** on Groceries was $322 in January and $255 in February, a total of $577. The **Average Amount Spent** is $577/2 = $288 (per month, rounded).

The **SUB-TOTAL** for **column 8** is $3471. That's $3917–$3471 = $446 less than the ***OVERALL TOTAL*** for the **MONTHLY Allocations**. That means $233 is available as the ½ EOM amount to put into each savings account. That is indicated by entering $223 as the **Amount Spent** for each savings account. The **Adjusted MONTHLY Allocations** are not shown. They are equal to the **Average Amounts Spent.**

Ideally, track your monthly spending for a full year. At the end of each month, add a column of **Amounts Spent** for that month**.** Some months will end up being overspent, others will be underspent. If a shortage happens at the end of the month, then use transfers from your savings accounts to cover it.

When a year has passed, for each Budget Category combine the **Amounts Spent** in the twelve columns to produce the year-long totals. Now you have **ANNUAL Amounts Spent** based on your actual history for an entire year. Sum them to get ***OVERALL TOTAL***.

If you have either underspent or overspent compared to your total **ANNUAL** Budget, then you must adjust the **ANNUAL Allocations** for the variable Budget Categories. You might adjust all of them or only adjust some of them and leave others unchanged. Either way, the result should be an ***OVERALL TOTAL*** equal to your total **ANNUAL** Budget.

One way to adjust those allocations is to proportion them all either downward or upward to achieve an ***OVERALL TOTAL*** equal to your total **ANNUAL** budget. For example, if you overspent your total **ANNUAL** budget, then decrease the **ANNUAL Allocation** for each variable Budget Category by the same percentage and that brings the ***OVERALL TOTAL*** to the correct amount. Conversely, if you overspent the total **ANNUAL** budget, then increase the **Allocation** for each variable Budget Category by the same percentage and that brings the ***OVERALL TOTAL*** to the correct amount.

By dividing all the resulting **ANNUAL Amounts Spent** by twelve, you produce <u>average</u> **MONTHLY Amounts Spent** for each Budget Category. Use them as the next year's **MONTHLY Allocations**. With that, your next budget flight takes off, repeat this process every year.

Quarterly Checkpoints

It might feel like waiting a full year to establish a realistic **ANNUAL** budget is a long period of time. It is. But once done you have made a big step. By the discipline developed in watching your monthly spending and being firm about depositing the fixed **MONTHLY Allocation** for Regular Savings and variable ½ EOM amount into your savings accounts every month you will accumulate cash steadily.

However, if you prefer, you can sum and average a series of **MONTHLY Amounts Spent** at intermediate points in time, e.g., every three months (quarterly). Each time use your **Adjusted MONTHLY Allocations** for the next quarter. At the end of the year, you will have very accurate **MONTHLY Allocations**. Multiply those amounts by 12 and use the results as the **ANNUAL Allocations** in a new budget table for the coming year.

Example 9

To illustrate a quarterly checkpoint let's add March to Table 10. **Columns 2-3** are unchanged from Table 9. Thus, they are omitted. Due to page width, the months of January, February and March are abbreviated in **columns 5, 6, and 7**.

TABLE 10

1		4	5	6	7	8	9
2020 BUDGET CATEGORIES		# of MONTHS	Amount Spent				Avg. Amt. Spent
		3	Ja	F	M	Jan-March	
FIXED							
Cable TV		114	38	38	38	114	38
Insurance-Auto		150	50	50	50	150	50
Insurance-Medical		951	317	317	317	951	317
Insurance-Dental		105	35	35	35	105	35
Insurance-Life		90	30	30	30	90	30
Internet		63	21	21	21	63	21
Reg. Savings		150	50	50	50	150	50
Rent		3350	1117	1117	1117	3350	1117
Cell Phone Service		150	50	50	50	150	50
VARIABLE							
Auto Fuel + Maintenance		750	321	277	218	816	272
Clothing		150	0	52	180	232	77
Computer Supplies		100	30	0	24	54	18
Dental		113	0	0	72	72	24
Dining + Entertainment		800	234	265	209	708	236
Eye Care		125	0	350	100	450	150
Gifts		150	0	0	51	51	17
Groceries		800	322	255	239	816	272

Home Maintenance And Repairs	**125**	**0**	**23**	**25**	**48**	**16**
Household	**150**	**77**	**55**	**18**	**150**	**50**
Laundry/Dry Cleaning	**38**	**15**	**0**	**17**	**32**	**11**
Liquor	**150**	**66**	**88**	**65**	**219**	**73**
Medical	**300**	**0**	**65**	**301**	**366**	**122**
Personal Care	**200**	**12**	**4**	**25**	**41**	**14**
Postage	**15**	**32**	**0**	**17**	**49**	**16**
Trash Service	**96**	**0**	**0**	**96**	**96**	**32**
Travel	**375**	**344**	**301**	**336**	**981**	**327**
Utilities	**700**	**144**	**56**	**283**	**483**	**161**
Miscellaneous	**293**	**77**	**63**	**58**	**198**	**66**
SUB-TOTAL	10152	3381	3561	4043	10985	3661
½ EOM to Primary Savings	**600**	**268**	**178**	**-63**	**383**	**128**
½ EOM to Rainy-Day Savings	**600**	**268**	**178**	**-63**	**383**	**128**
OVERALL TOTAL	*11351*	*3917*	*3917*	*3917*	*11751*	*3917*
2020 BUDGET CATEGORIES	3	Amount Spent				Avg. Amt. Spent
	# of MONTHS	Ja	F	M	Jan-March	
1	4	5	6	7	8	9

Table 10 has nine columns. **Column 4** indicates that Table 10 is for a three-month period. The listed values in **column 4** are the allocations for the three-month period. They are obtained by multiplying the **MONTHLY Allocations** entries in **column 3** by 3. The

Amounts Spent in each of the three months are listed in **columns 5, 6, and 7**. The **Amounts Spent** in **columns 5 and 6** are the same as in Table 9.

The combined **Amounts Spent** in each Budget Category for the three-month period are listed in **column 8**. They are obtained by summing the individual **Amounts Spent** in **columns 5, 6, and 7**. Dividing each result by 3 gives the **Average Amounts Spent** for the three-month period. Results are listed in **column 9**. For example, in March, the **Amount Spent** on Groceries was $239. Adding that amount to the January and February amounts, gives a total of $816. The **Average Amount Spent** monthly for the three-months period is $816/3 = $272 (per month).

The **SUB-TOTAL** for **column 9** is $3661 (per month). EOM = $3917 – $3661 = $256 (per month) That means $128 (per month) is available to put in each of the savings accounts. That is indicated by entering $128 as the **Average Amount Spent** for each savings account.

NOTE: For March, the **SUB-TOTAL** of the **Amounts Spent** ($4043) was greater than the **MONTHLY** take-home pay. As a result, EOM = $3917 – $4043 = –$126 and the **Amount Spent** for ½ EOM for each savings account is –$63. However, an adjustment is not necessary. That's because the combined **Amount Spent** for the three-month period is $383, a positive value. An adjustment would be necessary only if the combined result is negative.

These results present an opportunity for a quarterly look at the trend of the budgeted allocations. Table 11 illustrates how that is done. It partially repeats Table 10 and has the additional **columns 10 and 11**.

TABLE 11

1	3	8	9	10	11
2020 BUDGET CATEGORIES	MONTHLY Allocation	Amount Spent Jan-March	Avg. Amount Spent	MONTHLY Allocation – Avg. Amount Spent	Adjusted ANNUAL Allocation = 12 x Col. 9
FIXED					
Cable TV	38	114	38	0	456
Insurance-Auto	50	150	50	0	600
Insurance-Medical	317	951	317	0	3804
Insurance-Dental	35	105	35	0	420
Insurance-Life	30	90	30	0	360
Internet	21	63	21	0	252
Reg. Savings	50	150	50	0	600
Rent	1117	3350	1117	0	13400
Cell Phone Service	50	150	50	0	600
VARIABLE					

Auto Fuel + Maintenance	250	816	272	-22	3264
Clothing	50	232	77	-27	924
Computer Supplies	33	54	18	15	216
Dental	38	72	24	14	288
Dining + Entertainment	267	708	236	31	2832
Eye Care	42	450	150	-108	3264
Gifts	50	51	17	33	924
Groceries	267	816	272	-5	216
Home Maintenance + Repairs	42	48	16	26	288
Household	50	150	50	0	2832
Laundry/Dry Cleaning	13	32	11	2	3264
Liquor	50	219	73	-23	924
Medical	100	366	122	-22	216
Personal Care	67	41	14	53	2832
Postage	5	49	16	-11	3264
Trash Service	32	96	32	0	924
Travel	125	981	327	-202	216
Utilities	231	483	161	70	288
Miscellaneous	98	198	66	32	288
SUB-TOTAL	**3517**	**10983**	**3662**	**-145**	**43944**
½ EOM to Primary Savings	200	384	128	72	1536
½ EOM to Rainy-Day Savings	200	384	128	72	1536
OVERALL TOTAL	***3917***	***11751***	***3918***	***-1***	***47016***

2020 BUDGET CATEGORIES	*MONTHLY Allocation*	*Amount Spent Jan-March*	*Avg. Amount Spent*	*MONTHLY Allocation – Avg. Amount Spent*	Adjusted ANNUAL Allocation = 12 x Col. 9
1	3	8	9	10	11

Examining **column 8** indicates that money has been spent in every Budget Category. That was not the case either after one month or after two months.

The entries in **column 10** were obtained by subtracting the **Average Amount Spent** from the **MONTHLY Allocation** for each Budget Category. The results indicate by how much (on average for three months) each Budget Category was either underspent or overspent. For example, Personal Care was underspent by $53 (per month) and Postage was overspent by $11 (per month).

Entries in **column 11** were obtained for each Budget Category by multiplying each of the **Average Amounts Spent** by 12. The result is a quarterly projection of what the **ANNUAL Budget Allocations** would be if the **Average Amounts Spent** monthly for the first three months were the same after the next 9 months.

Example 10

After three more months pass, a second quarterly checkpoint can be done. Table 12 below illustrates that process. It extends the prior tracking to include the subsequent months April, May, and June (abbreviated A, M, and Ju) in **columns 6, 7**, and **8**. No changes were made to the **ANNUAL Allocations.** Thus, the **MONTHLY Allocations** are unchanged, too.

TABLE 12

1		4	5	6	7	8	9	10	11
2020 BUDGET CATEGORIES		# of MONTHS	Amount Spent					Avg. Amt. Spent	MONTHLY Allocation – Avg. Amount Spent
		6	Jan - March	A	M	Ju	Jan - June		
FIXED									
Cable TV		225	114	38	38	38	228	38	0
Insurance-Auto		300	.48	50	50	50	300	50	0
Insurance-Medical		1900	951	317	317	317	1991	317	0
Insurance-Dental		210	105	35	35	35	210	35	0
Insurance-Life		180	90	30	30	30	180	30	0
Internet		125	63	21	21	21	126	21	0
Reg. Savings		300	150	50	50	50	300	50	0
Rent		6700	3350	1117	1117	1117	6701	1117	0
Cell Phone Service		300	150	50	50	50	300	50	0
VARIABLE									
Auto Fuel + Maintenance		1632	816	121	204	180	1321	220	**30**
Clothing		462	232	312	0	180	724	121	**-71**

Computer Supplies	108	54	0	40	20	114	19	**14**
Dental	144	72	0	0	70	142	24	**14**
Dining + Entertainment	1416	708	214	272	210	1404	234	**33**
Eye Care	900	450	0	0	0	450	75	**-33**
Gifts	102	51	0	0	50	101	17	**33**
Groceries	1632	816	376	275	238	1705	284	**-17**
Home Maintenance And Repairs	96	48	123	159	25	355	59	**-17**
Household	300	150	43	65	17	275	46	**4**
Laundry/Dry Cleaning	66	32	0	22	16	70	12	**-1**
Liquor	438	219	45	100	65	429	72	**28**
Medical	732	366	118	57	300	841	140	**-40**
Personal Care	84	41	86	145	58	330	55	**12**
Postage	96	49	63	81	24	217	36	**-31**
Trash Service	192	96	7	24	17	144	24	**12**
Travel	1962	981	0	0	336	1317	220	**-95**
Utilities	966	483	296	266	281	1326	221	**12**
Miscellaneous	396	198	86	145	58	487	81	**17**
SUB-TOTAL	10152	10983	3598	3563	3853	21997	3668	-151
½ EOM to Primary Savings	768	384	*159*	177	32	752	125	**75**
½ EOM to Rainy-Day Savings	768	384	*159*	177	32	752	125	**75**
OVERALL TOTAL	23500	*11751*	*3916*	*3917*	*3917*	*23501*	*3918*	*-1*
2020 BUDGET CATEGORIES	6	Amount Spent					Avg. Amt. Spent	MONTHLY Allocation – Avg. Amount Spent
	# of MONTHS	Jan - March	A	M	Ju	Jan- June		
1	4	5	6	7	8	9	10	11

Column 4 indicates that 6 months of spending are included. That is because the additional three months

will be added to the results for January through March. The entries listed in **column 4** are obtained by multiplying each **MONTHLY Allocation** by 6.

Column 5 lists the combined **Amount Spent** for each Budget Category for the months January-March. They are taken from **column 8** of Table 10.

Columns 6-8 contain the individual **Amounts Spent** for each Budget Category in April, May, and June.

Column 9 lists the combined **Amounts Spent** for January-June. They are obtained by summing the amounts in **Columns 5-8** for each Budget Category. Dividing each result by 6 gives the **Average Amount Spent** for each Budget Category. Results are listed in **Column 10**. Though not listed, multiplying each by 12 would give the **Adjusted ANNUAL Allocations**.

Subtracting the **Average Amount Spent** for each Budget Category from the corresponding **MONTHLY Allocation** gives the results listed in **Column 11**. For example, Personal Care was underspent by $12 per month and Postage was overspent by $31 per month.

Example 11

This sequence is continued by tracking the next three months of spending. The only change in the process is that the number of months is 9 instead of 6. The following budget table shows the outcome. Again, the **MONTHLY Allocations** are unchanged and **columns 2 and 3** omitted.

TABLE 13

1	4	5	6	7	8	9	10	11
2020 BUDGET CATEGORIES	# of MONTHS	Amount Spent					Avg. Amt. Spent	MONTHLY Allocation – Avg. Amount Spent
	9	Jan - June	Jy	Au	S	Jan - Sept		
FIXED								
Cable TV	450	38	338	228	38	38	38	342
Insurance-Auto	600	50	450	300	50	50	50	450
Insurance-Medical	3800	317	2850	1901	317	317	317	2853
Insurance-Dental	420	35	315	210	35	35	35	315
Insurance-Life	360	30	270	180	30	30	30	270
Internet	250	21	187	126	21	21	21	189
Reg. Savings	600	50	450	300	50	50	50	450
Rent	13400	1117	10050	6701	1117	1117	1117	10052
Cell Phone Service	600	50	450	300	50	50	50	450
VARIABLE								
Auto Fuel + Maintenance	2250	1321	175	454	213	2163	240	10
Clothing	450	724	0	104	42	870	97	-47
Computer Supplies	300	114	0	0	36	150	17	16

Dental	338	142	0	0	70	212	24	14
Dining + Entertainment	2400	1404	302	478	312	2496	277	-10
Eye Care	375	450	0	0	0	450	50	-8
Gifts	450	101	64	0	51	216	24	26
Groceries	2400	1705	186	192	144	2227	247	20
Home Maintenance And Repairs	375	355	24	36	33	448	50	-8
Household	450	275	36	52	24	387	43	7
Laundry/Dry Cleaning	113	70	24	21	21	136	15	-3
Liquor	450	429	33	21	36	519	58	-8
Medical	900	841	0	0	15	856	95	5
Personal Care	600	330	42	66	24	462	51	16
Postage	45	217	24	0	12	253	28	-23
Trash Service	291	144	24	36	24	228	25	7
Travel	1125	1317	0	0	0	1317	146	-21
Utilities	2100	1326	204	224	312	2066	230	3
Miscellaneous	880	487	46	75	64	672	76	22
SUB-TOTAL	31652	21997	2892	3467	3141	31499	3501	16
½ EOM to Primary Savings	1800	752	512	225	388	1872	208	-8
½ EOM to Rainy-Day Savings	1800	752	512	225	388	1872	208	-8
OVERALL TOTAL	*35252*	*23501*	*3916*	*3917*	*3917*	*35243*	*3917*	*0*
2020 BUDGET CATEGORIES	9	Amount Spent					Avg. Amt. Spent	MONTH Allocation - Avg. Amount Spent
	# of MONTHS	Jan - June	Jy	Au	Sept	Jan - Sept		
1	4	5	6	7	8	9	10	11

In **column 4**, the number of months was changed from 6 to 9. Amounts listed in that column are obtained by multiplying each **MONTHLY Allocation** in **column 3** by 9.

Combined **Amounts Spent** for months January – June are taken from **column 9** of Table 12 and entered in **column 5**. Individual **Amounts Spent** for July, August, and September (Jy, Au, and S) are listed in **columns 6 – 8**. For each Budget Category, the **Amounts Spent** in **columns 5-8** are combined to obtain the cumulative **Amounts Spent** over the entire 9 months. Resulting amounts are listed in **column 9**. Dividing each by 9 gives the **Average Amounts Spent** listed in **column 10**.

The **Average Amounts Spent** constitute the **Adjusted MONTHLY Allocations** based on 9 months of tracking expenditures. Although not listed, multiplying each amount by 12 would give the **Adjusted ANNUAL Allocations**. The average amount by which each Budget Category is either underspent or overspent is listed in **column 11**.

Example 12

Repeating the sequence for 3 more months extends the tracking to the end of the year. The following budget table shows the outcome for hypothetical **Amounts Spent** for October, November, and December (O, N, and D).

TABLE 14

1	4	5	6	7	8	9	10	11
2020 BUDGET CATEGORIES	# of MONTHS	Amount Spent					Avg. Amount Spent	MONTH Allocation – Avg. Amount Spent
	12	Jan - Sept	O	N	D	Jan - Dec		
FIXED								
Cable TV	450	342	38	38	38	456	38	-1
Insurance- Auto	600	450	50	50	50	600	50	0
Insurance- Medical	3800	2853	317	317	317	3800	317	0
Insurance- Dental	420	315	35	35	35	420	35	0
Insurance- Life	360	270	30	30	30	360	30	0
Internet	250	189	21	21	21	202	21	0
Reg. Savings	600	450	50	50	50	600	50	0
Rent	13400	10052	1117	1117	1117	13400	1117	0
Cell Phone Service	600	450	50	50	50	600	50	0
VARIABLE								
Auto Fuel + Maintenance	3000	2163	96	144	324	2727	227	23
Clothing	600	870	0	42	0	912	76	-26
Computer Supplies	400	150	156	0	36	342	29	4
Dental	450	212	0	0	70	282	24	14
Dining + Entertain.	3200	2496	213	306	123	3138	262	5
Eye Care	500	450	0	0	0	450	38	4

Gifts	600	216	0	51	213	480	40	10
Groceries	3200	2227	144	162	240	2773	231	36
Home Maint. + Repairs	500	448	40	21	81	590	49	-7
Household	600	387	0	54	102	543	45	5
Laundry/Dry Cleaning	150	136	21	21	24	202	17	-5
Liquor	600	519	24	18	96	657	55	-5
Medical	1200	856	66	12	0	934	78	22
Personal Care	800	462	27	52	66	607	51	16
Postage	60	253	0	21	0	274	23	-18
Trash Service	388	228	36	24	24	312	26	6
Travel	1500	1317	0	0	0	1317	110	15
Utilities	2800	2066	186	213	282	2747	229	4
Misc.	1171	672	96	121	102	991	83	15
SUB-TOTAL	42200	31499	2813	2970	3491	40774	3401	116
½ EOM to Primary Savings	2400	1872	552	473	213	3110	259	-59
½ EOM to Rainy-Day Savings	2400	1872	552	473	213	3110	259	-59
OVERALL TOTAL	47002	*35243*	*3917*	*3917*	*3917*	*46994*	3919	-2
2020 BUDGET CATEGORIES	12	Jan - Sept	O	N	D	Jan - Dec	Avg. Amount Spent	MONTH Allocation – Avg. Amount Spent
	# of Months	Amount Spent						
1	4	5	6	7	8	9	10	11

The combined **Amounts Spent** for the entire year are listed in **column 9**. They constitute the **Adjusted**

ANNUAL Allocations for the start of the budget for the next year.

NOTE: The ***OVERALL TOTAL*** for Jan-December is $46994, $6 less than $47000. That small difference is due to rounding of numbers that was done throughout the calculations. To account for it, just add $6 to any of the individual categories.

NOTE: The combined amount of Regular Savings is $600. The combined amount of 1/2 EOM in each savings account is $3114. That is a total of $6228 that you saved that year.

Dividing the individual **Average Amounts Spent** by 12 gives the **Average Amount Spent** in each Budget Category. They constitute the **Adjusted MONTHLY Allocations** based on 12 months of tracking expenditures. The ***OVERALL TOTAL*** in **column 10** is $3919. The amount by which each Budget Category is either underspent or overspent is listed in **column 11**. Due to round-off of the individual amounts in the table, they sum to –$2 instead of $0.

Adjusted Allocations

In the above trail of quarterly budget checkpoints, the **ANNUAL Allocations** and **MONTHLY Allocations** remained unchanged in each checkpoint budget table. The amounts allocated initially were used throughout the sequence of checkpoints.

As an alternative, you might want to adjust the **MONTHLY Allocation** amounts at the start of each quarter. You do that by using the **Adjusted Allocations** that resulted at the end of the prior quarter.

The following budget table illustrates how to do that at the end of the first quarter. It is the revised budget table for the second quarter. Let's walk through it.

TABLE 15

1	2	3	4	5	6
2020 BUDGET CATEGORIES	Monthly Allocation	# of MONTHS	Amount Spent	Avg. Amount Spent	Monthly Allocation – Avg. Amount Spent
		6	Jan – June		
FIXED					
Cable TV	38	228	228	38	0
Insurance-Auto	50	300	300	50	0

Insurance-Medical	317	1900	1901	317	0
Insurance-Dental	35	210	210	35	0
Insurance-Life	30	180	180	30	0
Internet	21	125	126	21	0
Reg. Savings	50	300	300	50	0
Rent	1117	6700	6701	1117	0
Cell Phone Service	50	300	300	50	0
VARIABLE					
Auto Fuel + Maintenance	272	1632	1321	220	52
Clothing	77	462	724	121	-44
Computer Supplies	18	108	114	19	-1
Dental	24	144	142	24	1
Dining + Entertain.	236	1416	1404	234	2
Eye Care	150	900	450	75	75
Gifts	17	102	101	17	0
Groceries	272	1632	1705	284	-12
Home Maintenance + Repairs	16	96	355	59	37
Household	50	300	275	46	4
Laundry/Dry Cleaning	11	66	70	12	-1
Liquor	73	438	429	72	1
Medical	122	732	841	140	-18
Personal Care	14	84	330	55	-41
Postage	16	96	217	36	-60
Trash Service	32	192	144	24	8

Travel	327	1962	1317	220	107
Utilities	161	966	1326	221	-50
Misc.	66	396	487	81	-15
SUB-TOTAL	**3662**	**21964**	**21997**	**3668**	**-7**
½ EOM to Primary Savings	**128**	**768**	**752**	**125**	**32**
½ EOM to Rainy-Day Savings	**128**	**768**	**752**	**125**	**32**
OVERALL TOTAL	***3918***	***23500***	***23501***	***3918***	***-1***
2020 BUDGET CATEGORIES	Monthly Allocation	# of MONTHS	Amount Spent	Avg. Amount Spent	Monthly Allocation – Avg. Amount Spent
		6	Jan - June		
1	2	3	4	5	6

ANNUAL Allocations are omitted. **MONTHLY Allocations** are listed in **column 2**. Instead of retaining the initial **MONTHLY Allocations**, the listed amounts are taken as the **Average Amounts Spent** in the first quarter. They are taken from **column 10** of Table 12.

Column 3 indicates Table 15 covers 6 months. Amounts in that column are obtained by multiplying the **MONTHLY Allocations** by 6.

Amounts Spent in the individual months are omitted. They are the same as in Tables 10 and 12. The combined **Amounts Spent** for January through the June listed in **column 4** are taken from column 9 of Table 12. Dividing each by 6 gives the **Average Amount Spent** in each Budget Category. Subtracting each from the corresponding **MONTHLY Allocation** gives the amount by which each Budget Category was either underspent or overspent.

In **column 6**, the listed results for the variable Budget Categories differ from the previous results. For example, in Table 15 the allocation for Auto Fuel and Maintenance was underspent by $52. In Table 12 it was underspent by $30. The $22 difference is the consequence of the **MONTHLY Allocation** having been increased by $22, i.e., from the initial $250 to $272. Similarly, in Table 15 the **MONTHLY Allocation** for Clothing was overspent by –$44. In Table 12 it was overspent by –$71. The $27 difference is the consequence of the **MONTHLY Allocation** having been increased by $27, i.e., from the initial $50 to $77.

Notice that the **Average Amounts Spent** listed in Tables 12 and 15 for the various Budget Categories are identical. That's because the individual **MONTHLY Amounts Spent** are the same in both budget tables. There is an important implication. Here's why.

Adjusting the **MONTHLY Allocations** at the start of the second quarter made no difference in the **Average Amounts Spent**. At the end of the second quarter the **Average Amounts Spent** are the same in both budget tables. This will also occur in the succeeding quarters.

Based on that, it is apparent that to ***Create an Accurate Monthly Budget - On the Fly*** one need only track the cumulative **Amounts Spent** in each Budget Category from month to month. Dividing each of the cumulative **Amounts Spent** by the cumulative number of months gives the **Average Amounts Spent** to that point in time. Doing it each month, you gradually improve the estimate of the needed budget allocations. At the end of the year the **Average Amounts Spent** become the **MONTHLY Allocations** in the budget for the start of the next year.

As stated previously, without an accurate budget in place, spending money becomes an aimless, haphazard activity. Tracking only the **Amounts Spent** constitutes doing exactly that. The additional step of calculating the overspending and underspending allows one to observe spending habits and make any necessary or desired changes "on the fly". Adjusting all the **MONTHLY Allocations** to the **Average Amounts Spent** in the prior month (or quarter) is an automatic way of doing that. However, by looking at the overspent and underspent amounts in Budget Categories additional adjustments can be done.

For example, in Table 15, Travel was underspent by $107 per month (x 12 = $1284 per year). Perhaps, looking ahead, it is clear you will not be spending that much more. Also $50 per month (x 12 = $600 per year) more was spent on Utilities than allocated. Given that, you decide to decrease the **MONTHLY Allocation** for Travel by $50 per month and increase it for Utilities by $50 per month. Consequently, you change the **Adjusted MONTHLY Allocation** for Travel in the next quarter to $220 – $50 = $170 per month. To offset it you change the **Adjusted MONTHLY Allocation** for Utilities to $161 + $50 = $211 per month.

Just before the end of the second quarter, you also get a pay raise and your **MONTHLY** take-home pay increases by $80 per month. You want to account for it in your budget. You decide to add $20 per month to the **MONTHLY Allocation** of ½ EOM for each savings account. That increases the **Adjusted MONTHLY Allocation** for the next quarter to $125 + $20 = $145 per month. Noticing that Clothing was overspent by –$41 per month, you decide to allocate the remaining $40 per month to its **MONTHLY Allocation**. That increases the **Adjusted MONTHLY Allocation** for Clothing for the next quarter to $121 + $40 = $161 per month.

The result of these two actions are the following **MONTHLY Allocations** for the third quarter. The effects of the actions are shown in a larger font size. The rest of the table is unchanged.

TABLE 16

1	2
2020 BUDGET CATEGORIES	**MONTHLY Allocation**
FIXED	
Cable TV	**38**
Insurance-Auto	**50**
Insurance-Medical	**317**
Insurance-Dental	**35**
Insurance-Life	**30**
Internet	**21**
Regular Savings	**50**

Rent	1117
Cell Phone Service	50
VARIABLE	
Auto Fuel + Maintenance	220
Clothing	**161**
Computer Supplies	19
Dental	24
Dining + Entertainment	234
Eye Care	75
Gifts	17
Groceries	284
Home Maintenance and Repairs	59
Household	46
Laundry/Dry Cleaning	12
Liquor	72
Medical	140
Personal Care	55
Postage	36
Trash Service	24
Travel	**170**
Utilities	**221**
Miscellaneous	81
SUB-TOTAL	**3668**
½ EOM to Primary Savings	**145**
½ EOM to Rainy-Day Savings	**145**
OVERALL TOTAL	***3998***

NOTE: The ***OVERALL TOTAL*** of the **MONTHLY Allocations** has increased by $80 (from $3918 to $3998).

You may also find that you no longer need some Budget Categories and/or need to add some new ones. For example, you end cable TV service and replace it with an online streaming service. Or you take out a loan and must add the monthly payment to your fixed expenses. You can also reflect a rise in income by increasing some budget line items. If so, then make sure you add part of it to the allocation for Regular Savings.

That is the process for ***Creating an Accurate Monthly Budget –On the fly!*** The main point of this lesson is to illustrate how to go about gradually developing an accurate budget and use it effectively to control your saving and spending.

With basic ability in creating spreadsheets, you can create one for doing the calculations. That is how the author developed all the budget tables shown in this book. If needed, by searching Google and YouTube you can find many links to text and videos describing realistic budgets and how to construct one using spreadsheets. Likewise, you can locate apps that provide templates for creating a budget by filling in your own data and maintaining it on a monthly and/or annual basis.

If you work diligently on ***Creating an Accurate Monthly Budget –On the fly!*** then there is a big reward ahead. You were saving up for a well-deserved vacation escape and getting ready to **Fly Away! Fly Away! Fly Away!** *Your vacation flight has now taken off!!*

LESSON 7

The Budget Planning Retreat: Dialing Down the Stress Level in Money Matters

Developing a personal budget on the fly and annually adjusting it can be a mentally taxing, sometimes frustrating process. Every cubicle of projected expenses requires some portion of the available **MONTHLY** take-home pay. For fixed expenses, the allocations are set to known amounts and the only frustration is how much is left over after making those allocations. Setting the variable allocations requires judgment and the month by month and annual tracking of spending in those categories. In *LESSON 6* I explained how to go about that effectively. Now let's see how to take stress out of the budgeting process and decision-making!

Some of the variable Budget Categories are discretionary. Discretionary means they are non-essential (e.g., attending concerts) and including them or not and the amount of the **MONTHLY Allocation** to them are decisions to be made. Setting the amounts allocated to them can be trying. They cause the most challenge as those allocations are in a tug-of-war for the limited funds remaining after the **MONTHLY Allocations** to all the non-discretionary Budget Categories have been set.

Discretionary **MONTHLY Allocations** also involve some degree of emotional pull and wishful thinking. You might like to have $500 each month for dining out but can only allocate $300 each month. Some activities cannot be done at all; those having to be set at a zero allocation. For example, you might want to attend the NCAA Final Four basketball event but have no money to allocate for it in the Budget Category for Travel.

One would like to set all the discretionary allocations at the highest amounts possible. The reality is most of them must be set at allocations much less than one desires. There simply is not enough money remaining to allocate the desired amount to all of them.

When two people are involved in the family budget decision-making the challenge of doing it is heightened greatly. Each person imagines his or her own discretionary expense needs and relative sense of allocated amounts. For a husband and wife, he wants golf lessons, but she wants dance lessons, he wants an overseas vacation, and she wants a domestic trip. Those different wants magnify the tug-of-war process.

To minimize the stress and tension the author strongly recommends the use of a budget planning retreat. Here is how that is done.

The budget planning retreat should be held at a comfortable location in another town or city nearby. A nice hotel on a slow weekend for hotel traffic is an excellent choice. Minimize using the hotel room itself. The hotel should have a large enough atrium area or lobby area for finding a privacy spot. Comfortable seats and a table large enough to spread out items are musts. Some hotels offer rooms that have a table large enough to do that. If so, perhaps use it some of the time.

February is an excellent timing. All spending on credit and debit cards for the prior year have cleared. Other than at resorts and beach areas, hotel rates tend to be at their lowest rate. Pay for the retreat from the Rainy-Day Savings Account. If the saved funds are adequate, then you might travel by air to a more unique location.

Prepare in advance by compiling the budget information (**MONTHLY Allocations** versus **Average Amounts Spent**) for the past year. By ***Creating an Accurate Monthly Budget – On the Fly!*** the information is fully available already. Usually, one of the two people is responsible for this tracking and would have it nearly ready. He or she marks Budget Categories that were either overspent or underspent by noticeable amounts. Jointly review the expenditures for overspent categories. Make notations of the specific expenditures that led to each result. Noticeably underspent categories provide options to shore up the overspent ones.

Independently, each person develops his or her own wish list for discretionary expenses. List the items in order from highest to lowest priority. Annotate each with the applicable Budget Category and the tentative **MONTHLY Allocation** or its likely range. This should be completed in advance of the retreat.

Also prepare a list for short-term and/or long-term wants and needs that would require a large amount of money from the Rainy-Day Savings Account and/or Primary Savings Account. These would-be specific items and the estimated total amount of money needed.

Assemble the monthly bank statements for the **Primary Savings Account** and **Rainy-Day Savings Account**. Prepare a list of the major expenses paid from each of the accounts. Prepare a list of the monthly EOM amounts. The author does these on an ongoing basis by recording these costs each month.

Assemble any other documents to be taken to the retreat. For example, your most current income tax return and your medical expense file.

Many readers will want to utilize their laptop or notebook and electronic records at the retreat. I usually bring my laptop but only use it for limited referral. Subsequent writing and annotations are done on previously printed hard copies. That makes the retreat much more personal than having a financial interlude with a computer placed in between the two people.

Sometimes I do not bring my laptop. I never do when the retreat involves airline travel. That avoids having the retreat spreading to a prelude and epilogue unfolding at your plane seats. I use the flights to rest, as I want to start fresh after I arrive at the retreat location and after I return home.

DAY 1:

After arrival at the hotel, have an early lunch. Then move to a private location. "Walk through" the budget material from the past year, pausing at Budget Categories that were marked as either overspent or underspent and look at the notations as to why. Discuss the likelihood of each occurring again.

Take a break and walk around for 10-15 minutes. Over coffee or drinks, use the rest of that afternoon to again walk through the Budget Categories that are either overspent or underspent. Jointly settle on a trial, revised dollar range for each of them. Annotate these on a copy of the previous year's budget sheets. You might have to add some Budget Categories and remove others. For example, you might have taken out and/or paid off a loan. Also mark all known or anticipated changes to the fixed expenses. For example, an increase in rent or a decrease in an insurance cost.

Once done, enjoy the evening apart from the budget process.

MORNING OF DAY 2:

After breakfast, discuss the individual wish lists for discretionary expenses. Take turns. In each turn discuss a single item from your wish list in the order of indicated priorities. If they are not prioritized, then just pluck one off your list. That tends to happen impromptu anyway, as also does a tendency to alternate between easy items and difficult ones. Explain the motivation and the basis for the tentative allocated amount or range for each selected item. Do not debate them. That comes later. Some items might appear on both lists. The combined range can be used as the tentative one.

Take a few minutes to independently reconsider one's own order of priorities and possibly adjust them. Then compile the results into a single wish list, in alternating order of each person's priorities. If needed, toss a coin to determine who goes first. Transfer the range of the allocated amounts from the wish list as annotations to the copy of the previous year's budget sheet. Assign them to the applicable Budget Categories. If necessary, assign them to a new Budget Category. And, if applicable, remove Budget Categories that are no longer needed.

Sum up the trial **MONTHLY Allocation** amounts twice, once for the low values of the ranges and once for the high values of the ranges. The result is your first trial budget and the range of the ***OVERALL TOTAL*** for the **MONTHLY** Budget. Compare the ***OVERALL TOTAL*** with the current **MONTHLY** take-home pay. The result will bring a reaction which can range from broad smiles to overheard gasps. Regardless of the reactions, stop!

Have lunch on the premises or nearby, but away from the budgeting area (especially if it is becoming a combative arena) and the subject matter. Adjust mindsets as to actions needed next.

AFTERNOON OF DAY 2:

Once feeling renewed, return to the budgeting area. Review the trial budget range for each Budget Category and overall results determined that morning. Spend time in an initial give and take about the budget amounts. In mid-afternoon take a break for either coffee or wine or snacks or a stroll outdoors. Upon returning, chat and settle on agreeable allocated amounts (specific amounts, not ranges) for as many Budget Categories as possible and to the extent possible. For Budget Categories with troublesome amounts, agree to "sleep on it." After an evening dinner out or pizza in the room, do exactly that.

MORNING OF DAY 3:

Have breakfast in the hotel room. Mid-morning, start again and resolve the allocated amounts for the troublesome Budget Categories.

All allocated amounts are annotated on a second copy of the previous year's budget. The total must equal the available take-home pay. If not, then adjust.

Next, discuss each item on the list for short-term and/or long-term needs and wants. Determine how each will be addressed. For each "need" (non-discretionary) item decide whether funds will be taken from either the Primary Savings Account or the Rainy-Day Savings Account or from both. Once done, determine if the remaining funds exceed the target amount. If so, the "smell the roses" overage is available for the listed "want "(discretionary) items. Jointly discuss them and decide which, if any, "wants" can and will be covered by the overage amount.

Consider whether a separate savings account is needed for any long-term need/want and the feasibility of establishing one. If so, then add a Budget Category for it below the **SUB-TOTAL** row of your budget table. For example. You might add a row for a New Car Savings Account. Then decide what portion of the EOM funds are to go into that savings account each month. For example, you might decide to put 20% of the EOM amount into it each month. Then 40% goes into each of the base savings accounts.

Finally, reevaluate the desired target amounts for the Primary Savings Account and the Rainy-Day Savings Account, and set one for, in this example, for the New Car Savings Account.

You are now done, so put the stuff away. Check out of the hotel. Enjoy the rest of the day and the trip home.

AFTERWARDS:

During the following week, the main budget tracker formalizes the new budget in a computer file. You then discuss it in a mini retreat of a half-day at your favorite quiet local place and confirm or tweak the **MONTHLY Allocation** for each Budget Category.

RAINY-DAYS:

From time to time during the year, financial Rainy-Days arise. Those should also be discussed and resolved away from home. Having a mini retreat for a few hours over coffee or drinks at your favorite quiet location should suffice to come to a mutual conclusion. Indeed, for any financial matter requiring a significant decision, I advise "Never discuss significant money matters at home. Always get away to a quiet public location." By doing so it is highly unlikely that tempers and emotions will flare up.

By using the described cooperative approaches, joint budgeting will be accomplished calmly and effectively. Conflicting individual priorities will be resolved mutually in a non-combative manner. When surprise high-cost expenditures spring up, you will take them in stride and handle them calmly and peacefully. Now, being buoyed and encouraged, decide the timing for your first budget planning retreat and mark the dates on your calendars!

CLOSING

Going broke is something that no one wants to experience. Being penniless is a very unpleasant situation. It is terrifying to be there. In this primer I have shared my path for avoiding that place.

Saving and budgeting money are the keys to avoiding running out of it. Doing them well allows you to live life more comfortably, with less worries than you would have otherwise. Being fit financially and mentally leads to enjoying that Kentucky Derby, or that trip to Hawaii and other wishful thinking wants in your life. I want you to be able to smell such roses.

I want you to get past any mental roadblocks to consistently saving and budgeting money and onto the path of doing it and doing it well. Here is my process in a nutshell.

My Golden Rule of Saving: Pay Yourself Last, But Always Pay Yourself Something! is the starting line. Along the path, you will gradually develop your budget and systematically implement changes over time. I termed that ***Creating an Accurate Monthly Budget – On the fly!***

At the finish line, a relaxed *Budget Managing Retreat* awaits you. It will change budgeting from a mundane activity without excitement to a mix of fun and productive activity. While sorting out discretionary money matters is the focus, you will be in a comfortable place outside the home and have intermittent and overnight break times at hand. The rest and relaxation and time to think and sleep on tough choices and decisions is a boon to success.

Working on budgeting each month might seem like it will wear you down. Frankly, it can. My wife and I faced that consternation in the first year and had to push through it. In the coming year with more accurate **ANNUAL Budget Allocations,** it became a task to be done every other month or so. In time, it evolved to doing it only once or twice per year. It became evident that just a few variable budget categories dominated the discretionary budget. In our case they were groceries, dining out, home maintenance, lawncare, liquor, and Christmas gifts. Controlling those had the biggest effect on our spending.

Periodically, medical/dental expenses spiked but

were taken care of via medical insurance and money accumulated in our Rainy-Day Savings Account. Travel costs for extended vacation trips were also significant but were planned for on an annual or bi-annual basis and consideration of the money available in our Rainy-Day Savings Account. Spending on fixed expense categories required only small tweaks.

If you have a child bound for a college campus, then you will be including educational costs in your **MONTHLY Allocations**. And saving extra for those in a separate Budget Category will start well before he or she walks on to a college campus. Alongside that early start, you will encounter your kid begging for that credit and or debit card! The day will come when he/she needs a car (new or used). By reading my other primers and extended books you will be on the path to helping and teaching him/her all about those needs and handling oncoming money and debt matters in general.

I express my deepest appreciation to **Hannah Musgrave,** for her heartfelt and thorough reviewing of drafts of this book. As a college student majoring in Communications at Colorado State University she was the reader for all the drafts. She also created the cartoons used throughout the book. Her input, critique, editing, and discussions with me were invaluable in completing the project in a professionally solid manner.

Thank you for reading **How To Avoid Going Broke! A PRIMER *for Parents and Their Teenagers***. You have taken an important step on the path of preparing your child to handle debt well! Hopefully, you will consider also reading the predecessor book ***How To Borrow Money! Handle Credit! Repay Debt!*** **BASIC LESSONS *for Parents and Their Children***. Forthcoming primers will cover the basics of other specific topics from my at-length books. I encourage you to access them and share them as you progress the different stages of your child's need for your help with monetary matters.

May I ask for your help? Reviews are very helpful to improving future books. If you found **How To Avoid Going Broke! A PRIMER *for Parents and Their Children***. informative and helpful, please review the book on Amazon. It takes a just a few minutes, so please do it while it is fresh on your mind. In fact, please do it right now, before returning to your busy life and having it slip away.

Please Note:

The content of this book reflects the author's personal approaches, methods, experiences, thought processes, observations, and strategies. He is not a financial planner. Professional financial planning advisors might see some things similarly, others differently.

All numerical work was done carefully and rechecked several times but is not infallible. It is the reader's responsibility to confirm the calculated numbers. If in doing that doubts arise, then please feel free to contact the author (via his website) about questioned values. He will either confirm the calculated values or correct them.

Fictional settings are used in this book. Similarities to real people, places or events are entirely coincidental. The anecdotes about the author, his daughter, and his wife in the *Background* and *Closing* are exceptions. They are factually true.

About *Matthew Rich*

Matthew Rich is a pen name for Richard M. Gutkowski. Richard is a caring parent, grandparent, and educator. As frequent nanny-like babysitters, he and his wife thoroughly enjoy their two toddler grandchildren. Albeit constantly energetic boys and at times challenging, it is rewarding to watch and be part of their growth. One day they will be teenagers and, hopefully, learning a lot from his writings.

His experience includes a dedicated career as a professor teaching and advising college students. He involved many of them in research projects and their associated budgets. Globally, he managed numerous professional workshops and conferences. In those capacities he managed budgets totaling millions of dollars.

He transferred his highly developed professional fiscal skills into managing his family's home finances. Over time discipline, wise financial decision-making, astute financing principles and strategic borrowing methods became his forte.

Richard earned B.S and M.S. degrees in civil engineering from Worcester Polytechnic Institute, and a Ph.D. in structural engineering from the University of Wisconsin, Madison. An Emeritus Professor at Colorado State University, he wrote over 160 refereed technical papers and reports and STRUCTURES: Fundamental Theory and Behavior. He still reviews journal articles and grant applications in his field for publishers and research agencies world-wide.

Richard resides in beautiful Fort Collins, Colorado. As breaks from his writing and self-publishing, he enjoys hiking mountain trails, dining out, Happy Hours, weekend getaways, and the physical challenges and life extending benefits of CrossFit training. Above all, he treasures time with his family including his buddy Warhol, the grandkids' adorable, tiny, black Chihuahua who seems to favor him and sleeps snuggled beside him on every overnight stay.

Reach him at:

Web site: https//:www.debtisafourletterword.net

Facebook:www.facebook.com/richard.m.gutkowski/

https://www.youtube.com/channel/UCSieSG7BTLCFToHuqvSX

How to Borrow Money! Handle Credit! Repay Debt!

BASIC LESSONS *for Parents and Their Children*

By Matthew Rich

This primer covers the basics parts, nuts, and bolts of generally taking on formal debt and how it is repaid. It illustrates the problems created when debt is either not properly repaid or unscrupulous circumstances exist in the terms of a loan. The monetary aspects of taking on and repaying debt from credit cards are explained. The repayment of "amortized" loans is explained and illustrated via numerical examples.

Comprised of 7 Lessons. (63 pages)

Available on Amazon

DEBT is a Four-Letter Word - *But it Need Not Be!*

THE COLLEGE EXPERIENCE

By Richard M. Gutkowski. Ph.D., P.E.

Written in narrative style, fictional Nicole and her Dad navigate through her need for a credit card for ongoing college expenses, financing her college dreams, considering graduate school, and planning for post-graduation repayment of student loans. Nicole's walk began with her enthusiastic, teenaged plea for a credit card. It ends with her debt due to the costs of college successfully managed. Equally important, the reader observes the non-monetary aspects of how Nicole's Dad interacted with her caringly and effectively.

Comprised of 20 LESSONS, 42 realistic SITUATIONS and 39 accompanying practical EXERCISES. *(263 pages)*

Available on Amazon

DEBT is a Four-Letter Word - *But it Need Not Be!*
THE CAR FINANCING EXPERIENCE
By Richard M. Gutkowski. Ph.D., P.E.

The reader continues to walk along with Nicole and her advisor Dad as she faces a challenge not uncommon to young college graduates. Ever since her sweet sixteen old birthday, she has been driving a parent-provided, low-cost car. Now she needs to replace that long-used, undependable car. And, for the first time, she must do it herself. Dad helps her learn about the car purchasing, car loans, car leasing and car brokering processes and car insurance. In the end, armed with that knowledge and acting on her own, Nicole makes an informed and surprising choice in acquiring her new car.

Comprised of 14 LESSONS, the book covers 29 realistic SITUATIONS and 29 parallel practical EXERCISES. *(241 pages)*

Available on Amazon

Originally written by Jimmy Cox, there are many written versions of the lyrics for Nobody Knows You When You're Down and Out. It was first recorded by Bessie Smith. The following are the lyrics of her rendition.

Once I lived the life of a millionaire
Spending my money, I didn't care.
I carried my friends out for a good time,
Buying bootleg liquor, champagne and wine.

Then I began to fall so low,
I didn't have a friend, and no place to go
So if I ever get my hand on a dollar again
I'm gonna hold on to it till them eagle's grin

Nobody knows you when you down and out
In my pocket not one penny
And my friends I haven't any
But If I ever get on my feet again
Then I'll meet my long lost friend
It's mighty strange, without a doubt
Nobody knows you when you down and out
I mean when you down and out

Mmm, when you're down and out
Mmm, not one penny
And my friends I haven't any
Mmm, well I felt so low
Nobody wants me round their door
Mmm, without a doubt
No man can use you when you down and out
I mean when you down and out

"Nobody Knows You When You're Down and Out Lyrics." Lyrics.com. **STANDS4 LLC, 2020. Web. 23 Jun 2020. <https://www.lyrics.com/lyric/226033/Bessie+Smith>.**

Made in the USA
Monee, IL
18 September 2025

26010446R00080